INTRODUCTION

S everal years ago, late in my investment career, I was speaking with a friend and very successful investor, sharing stock ideas. When I finished detailing my favorite idea of the moment, he responded, "That is so your style," to which I replied, "What are you talking about? I don't have a style." This evoked a pretty big laugh, and he said, "You must be kidding. You have the most obvious style I have ever seen." After I challenged him to describe it, he responded, "That's easy: Greg against the world."

At the time, that really put me back on my heels. This is not how investors talk or how they would ever describe an investment style. We have very specific language for all that in the industry. But he saw beyond the conventional. He saw how my clock really ticked.

For a long time, I buried that remark as a humorous, even flattering, comment; not until I began writing this story did I revisit it. Now, with a different vantage point, I thought about that statement for a long time before conceding its truth. Not only was he right but he also understood me more clearly than I understood myself. Somehow, someplace, I had substituted confidence for hubris, competition for conflict, independence for detachment, and conviction for certainty. I don't want to be too unyielding in my self-appraisal. I certainly was always kind, considerate, compassionate, and capable. But in some weird way, that is what I expected of myself. There was no choice. This other characterization was addressing something apart from what I expected of myself. It was my preference, a making of my own free choice. I wanted this, yet as I read these words for the first time, I ask myself, "Why?" Quite frankly, I don't have an answer.

By all accounts, my career on Wall Street was a success. For over twenty years, I managed client capital and produced a record of performance that far exceeded the majority of my peers. I was a partner in four different investment firms, was extremely active in the charitable world, and, in general, was well liked and respected. Yet, as I looked back, I was filled with disappointment. I was jealous of those whom I felt accomplished so much more. I was jealous of those who were recognized for their accomplishments. I was disappointed because I failed to realize my expectations and goals. And I was disappointed that it all ended far

IT'S A MATTER OF TRUST

How trust changes every risk you take and every decision you make

Greg Lewin

ISBN: 1546445390
ISBN 13: 9781546445395

For my loving wife and family

too soon because of my misplaced senses of ego and pride. As I drifted from disappointment toward depression, my personal crisis was amplified by a serious health event. From that point forward, things began to unwind very quickly.

It's a strange thing to be in your fifties without a road map to guide your way. You build your life on a series of assumptions, and very few seem to apply going forward. I was brought up to be completely self-reliant, fiercely independent, and proudly different, but suddenly, I had the sneaking suspicion that I needed to learn new ways. I had constructed a personal narrative of mental, physical, and emotional strength and I was ready to withstand punishment. In fact, I regularly sought punishment to test my constitution. However, I began to realize that the way forward required an entirely new approach that emphasized self-kindness and compassion. I had sought very competitive operating environments in work and play to constantly push and measure myself. Now I realized that I needed to stop measuring. And even though my life choices sound harsh, I liked them, and now I needed to learn to like very different things. But more than anything, I needed to learn a whole new way to process failure because that was the feeling that was consuming me twenty-four/seven.

A good friend and advisor once counseled that the less important question is: "What have you learned?" The far more fundamental question is: "Are you ready to learn?" Without a particular plan or purpose, I had embarked on a twenty-year period of study that, fortunately, dissected this period of personal crisis. And although I had gained a great deal of knowledge, I soon understood that I had come no closer to wisdom. I simply was not ready. It was only in the heat of an extended period of personal distress that I began to melt my meticulously forged protective shell of personal belief. With my protection made vulnerable, I finally put myself in a position to begin again, and for the first time, I introduced the prospect of learning what needed to be learned.

This story began as an exercise in personal therapy and evolved into an education that changed my life. This is a story about trust, and the ways in which it influences the risks we take and the decisions we make. Trust is one of the prime moving factors influencing the directions of our lives. In Part 1, I look back on my life in search of the answer to a very simple, straightforward question: "How did so much go so wrong when everything was going so right?" When all that I aspired to accomplish was within reach, why did I do my best to undermine my future? Following some poor choices, my work prospects dimmed along with my physical and mental health. When I finally summoned the willpower to climb out of my well-fortified bunker, the very first thing I did was re-examine my life from the very beginning. The answers were back there and I just needed to find them.

This is not a memoir. Many of the most important people and events in my life are given little attention or, in many cases, no attention at all. My intention is to share the significant developmental experiences and relationships that created the foundation of my personal relationship with trust. What I eventually discovered was that my relationship with trust shaped my entire life and until very recently, I was completely unaware of this fundamental truth.

Identifying the answers to my questions was only the first step. If I really wished to change my life, I needed to turn trust from a liability to an asset. In Part 2, I begin the mental and physical work necessary to become ready to learn. I begin to explore new thoughts and strategies for repair and growth. And most importantly, I begin to take risks and make choices to change the direction of my life.

Finally, in Part 3, I shift from my personal journey of discovery to my greater journey toward understanding. I dissect the subject of trust into fundamentally digestible pieces, offering observations and examples that provide evidence of the power of trust. From there I move on to explore the intrinsic nature of trust and the many ways it changes our lives. Our relationship with trust is a struggle and there are many forces aligned to undermine its healthy balance. I discuss some of these factors and provide some strategies to help the reader enlist this force of human nature to better navigate risk-taking, improve decision-making and elevate their capacity to trust.

I hope this story brings you closer to a place where great learning is possible.

PART 1

BEGININGS

B y all accounts, things were a bit different to start. We were an ultraliberal, Jewish family living in a mostly black school district in the racially charged 1960s and 1970s. This was not the cool-to-hang-with black crowd. This was the aggressive, angry, in-your-face crowd. Different groups kept to themselves, and boundaries were enforced with intimidation and violence. And to make the situation all the more combustible, the second-largest group was comprised of newly immigrated Italians. English was often a second language, and affiliation with the Mafia was not uncommon. These two groups absolutely hated each other—to the point where intergroup violence was pretty rare because everyone understood that the consequences were potentially explosive. Being a white, middle-class Jew in this poor to lower-middle-class ethnic community put me somewhat on an island. It was important that I kept most of the details of my life, like being Jewish or being part of a family that could afford to go on a yearly vacation, to myself, because these differences could easily be exploited, and I had no group to fall back on for protection.

We moved to Westbury, Long Island, in 1957, the year of my birth. We lived in a modest $23,000 home, purchased with a $13,000 down payment that consumed all of the savings from my father's military service and my mother's modest income working as a school teacher in Maine. My father was a dentist, and after going further into debt to buy equipment for his office, we lived on the edge of bankruptcy for the first couple of years. There was really no one in our extended family in a position to provide financial assistance. During my father's time in the military, my mother had quit college to help with the finances. Now pregnant, she started selling homemade crafts from the house and worked as his receptionist and general helper in his office. She wasn't very good with the sight of blood, so her work as his assistant wasn't destined to last long.

Although one might assume that being a dentist was a road to prosperity, but that was not necessarily the case when servicing an economically challenged community. Fees charged were exceedingly modest and failure to pay bills was common practice, but no one was ever turned away from service. Eventually it was the Mafia that saved my father's practice and formed the foundation of a much more profitable future—but we will attend to that part of the story later.

We lived in a wonderful, multiethnic housing development of thirty homes, owned equally by Greeks, Italians, Cubans, and Jews. Generally speaking, everyone was in the same boat starting out: modest means and two, three, or four kids per family, all roughly two years apart. We were very much defined by our unique geography in the far corner of town, cut off from the rest by two extremely busy highways and a popular strip mall that included a fantastic bakery, a candy store we all lived for, an old-fashioned barbershop, and a somewhat gross grocery store.

I lived at One Greentree Circle, right on Jericho Turnpike. And after the government annexed our backyard to expand the highway from four lanes to six, we were forever wed to the road, with its noise, traffic, and peculiar number of fatal accidents. The road was always busy, and given our location—relative to the strip mall and an ill-placed traffic light—a large number of fatal accidents took place right in front of our home. Whether I was outside, bouncing a ball, or inside the house, that familiar sound of screeching tires and the inevitable thud that followed drew me to the street immediately. More often than not, the victims never got up again. My neighbor was eventually included among those who died on that stretch of road. It wasn't until many years later that I took a moment to explore this particular oddity of my youth. I asked my mother, "How many people did I see who were struck by cars and, on many occasions, die?" She guessed twenty, and my recollection was not meaningfully different. By no means did this define me or determine who I was to become, but it certainly was a strange way to start.

Life on Greentree Circle was actually fantastic and, by all accounts it was a great place to grow up. Friends were abundant, doors were largely unlocked, and sports were nonstop. We all rode our bikes everywhere; gathered to play football and basketball daily; organized endless games of Monopoly, Ping-Pong, and pool; ran for the Good Humor truck on Saturdays; and participated in Sunday-night ring-a-levio. Because we lived above a dentist office on the highway, we were robbed three times, mostly for the drugs in the office. But those things never bothered me. I always felt very safe and secure on the Circle. We knew people of different backgrounds and cultures, and we were largely on our own from a very young age.

Kids hung out together from ages eleven through eighteen, and everyone was welcome. We were equal-opportunity friendly, competitive, abusive, and gender neutral. And, although we were generally left on our own, every mother in the neighborhood would call your mom in a nanosecond if you did something out of line. In most cases, the embarrassment and punishment that followed were sufficient enough to dissuade repeat offenders, excepting the few psychos that roamed among us. Overall, Greentree Circle was a bit of a throwback to a time gone by—a real community, where neighbors cared about, complained about, and helped one another. Yet amid this fifties-style neighborhood, we existed very much within the confines of a racially explosive town of the sixties.

The elementary school we attended was over 90 percent black, and no one noticed until Martin Luther King, Jr. was killed. From then on, protests, riots, and violence were part of the daily ritual throughout the school system. I remember my first taste of the violence when riots broke out at the high school. One of the older boys in the neighborhood went to investigate and came home with a broken arm. From then on, you could feel the divide in the community grow. Road closures, marches, school closures, and random acts of violence were simply parts of the landscape. I even remember Walter Cronkite broadcasting a national story about racial violence and protests, using our high school as the backdrop.

As we aged into middle school, things changed. The violence was becoming more personal. When a girl was raped in a hallway during school hours, my parents decided to make a change. They bought a small plot of land in the neighboring town of Jericho, a safe, affluent, Jewish school district known for academic excellence, and sent my sister there to finish school. Because I was a boy, they gave me a choice. I didn't hesitate for a second. I was staying.

I still remember my simple thought process: Why did all those kids get to drive Cadillacs to school, when the kids in Westbury had so little? In those days the Cadillac was the symbol of privilege and wealth, and although I didn't resent wealth—because, quite frankly, I was not exposed to it—I did resent the kids who were advantaged by wealth simply because of their good fortune. Even at this young age I knew, without any hesitation, that if I was so privileged I would be embarrassed to draw any attention or to make others feel less fortunate. I always saw through the eyes of the disadvantaged, and I had little tolerance for those who did not share my perspective.

Though in more ways than one I was far more like the kids in Jericho than the kids in Westbury, I could not have felt more different. And because all of the kids in my neighborhood didn't share these feelings, and because many would not have made the choice to stay, I think now is a great time to introduce my parents to add background and context to my decision.

FAMILY

My father was a simple man, and I mean that in all the best ways. He was quiet, but when he spoke, he commanded our undivided attention. He was hardworking and dependable to a fault, and most of all, he was comfortable with himself. He never measured himself relative to others nor found any use for gossip or boasting. He lived his life by the values he held close, regardless of the views of others. And although he was not emotionally expressive, the love we all felt was warm and unwavering.

All of us completely understood that we could count on Dad; we just did not call for his attention very often. He was unquestionably our center of gravity. And although we appreciated all he did for us, he didn't require our acknowledgement. His disposition was that of a serious man with things to do and problems to solve. His role was central, but his voice and presence were understated. And that's just the way he liked it.

When Dad opened his dental practice he was broke and the banks were unwelcoming. My parents had to count on the generosity of relatives for help with groceries and other necessities of life. So when Aunt Annette found out Mom had one pair of shoes with a hole in the bottom, she immediately took her to the store to get a second pair. These first experiences really left a powerful imprint on Dad. He was determined never to be dependent on others again. He lived modestly and never borrowed again. He would always say to me, "If you can't do something the way you want to, then don't do it at all." And very often he simply chose to do without.

In the early days, Dad was pretty stressed about money and worked long hours to make ends meet. One of the unfortunate side effects of his disposition and schedule was that Dad and I didn't talk very much while I was growing up. I'll never forget in my late twenties when I walked into a room where he was watching baseball. We never watched baseball in our family. In fact, I don't remember Dad ever coming to one of my little league games. When I asked why he was watching, he replied, "I used to play a little." After further inquiry, he told me that he used to play regularly with Frank and Joe Torre, and that he pitched for the Brooklyn Dodgers minor-league baseball team. I was blown away. And when I asked why he didn't stick with it or mention it before, he simply replied, "I wasn't any good, and I had to get on with school and earn a living." After Dad passed away, I could not recall whether he had played for the double-A or triple-A team. When I asked Mom for some clarification, she had none to offer, commenting, "Who cares? It's a stupid game anyway."

Dad was a product of a tough Brooklyn neighborhood, extremely stern parents, and a father who traveled constantly to earn a living. As a result, he developed a tough exterior and a rather firm style. It was never difficult to know exactly where he stood. There were few things he felt worthy of his opinion, but should he choose to offer one, he was crystal clear. He always reminded me to never judge a man when he was up, only when he was down. He was extremely dismissive of any displays or boasts of success or wealth. He admired hard work, he admired tenacity, and he respected those who chose to keep their accomplishments to themselves. Simplicity, honesty, and dependability were his barometers of worth. In general, he found himself culturally very misplaced in the suburbs of New York. But his penchant for modesty and his straightforward style made Dad a real man's man, which turned out to be very appealing to our neighbors.

There were two guys in our neighborhood connected to the Mafia, both in positions of real power. In fact, our neighbor was featured in a story about the Mafia in *Newsday* (one of the large New York-area daily newspapers) and his picture was plastered on the entire back page of that particular issue of the paper. These guys loved Dad. Mom would periodically get nervous, but it never bothered Dad. He took the guys out golfing and let them win; he was a terrific golfer. And, most importantly, they provided a steady stream of good-paying patients for my father's practice when he most needed them. Mom later confessed that without their help, we may possible have not made it. They were also a source of great discounts on new cars when guys were in need of some quick cash. For me, they were simply nice old men whom I called names as they chased me around the yard. But there was one episode that reminded us all that they were different.

My father had bought a small house that he rented as an investment property. After several years, he received an offer to buy the house and gave the renter three months' notice. Well, renters have a lot of power in New York, and dislodging them can be tricky. As time marched on, my father became worried that he was going to lose the sale. Then, Dominic heard about the problem. The next day, three men showed up at the renter's house. Dad got a call that day from the obstinate tenant, assuring him that he would be out by 11:00

a.m. The sale went through, and we never heard a peep from anyone.

After I left for college, Dad's business turned a corner, resulting in a changed level of financial security along with a meaningfully easier disposition. The first time he called me at college, I was caught completely off-guard. At first, simple conversation was a real struggle for us both, but with time and practice, things became easier. In the years that followed, a real funny side began to emerge from my father, which made our time together a joy. With the passing of time, when grandchildren finally arrived, evidence of his old, stern self was hard to find, and this is how I choose to remember him.

My memories of Dad are overwhelmingly positive. His balance of honesty, dependability and decency overwhelmed any shortcomings attributable to his economy of emotional availability. From him I inherited a dislike for gossip and boastful behavior, a sense of modesty and a lack of concern for what others thought of me. He was truly happy with his life and never looked back with any sense of regret. His ease was infectious.

But if there was one characteristic that I wish had not leached into my character, it was the ease with which Dad summarily dispatched with those who did not share the things he valued most. Common disagreements of opinion were perfectly acceptable. But if he determined you were self-absorbed, a braggart or a person lacking in character, he was done. There was no anger or need for confrontation; he simply wrote you off and never looked back. For the longest time I also embraced this posture. I had my list, and if others did not measure up, I had no interest in wasting a single moment of time or ounce of energy. But now I look back and ask, "At what cost?" Maybe the self-absorbed person was a brilliant thinker or the braggart a truly generous soul. I would never know. *My inflexible nature and uncompromising attitude often led me to go it alone rather than invest my trust in others.*

Mom is a much different story. She is of the big-personality mold. She turned her home-based crafts business into a cottage interior-decorating business. She went back to Queen's College to finish her degree (which, she never fails to remind us, was free) and then transformed the business into a very large and successful decorating and design enterprise. She loves to work and logged five days a week up until her early eighties. She has a striking look and an independent personality that attracts a lot of attention.

Mom grew up in Brooklyn and Queens to loving, unconventional parents. The family moved every couple of years to new apartments in new neighborhoods, but this was never a problem for her. Since the age of thirteen, she always had a job; she made her own clothes and used her money to go into Manhattan to take dance lessons from Martha Graham. She knew all the great dancers of the time, and between dance and art, as she would say, "I was never bored." And, although my mom was a true free spirit who loved spending time in Greenwich Village with the artists, she was a real prude. She never used foul language, you could never speak badly of others, and we never spoke of nor kidded about anything sexual in the house. In fact, my father's nickname for Mom was "Virgin Mary." Nothing could better illustrate the suitability of this name than one of her earlier jobs at the New York Public Library. Mom was put in charge of the pornography cage because the managers knew she would never look at the books and magazines, and she never did.

Nothing was ever too difficult and nothing was ever too much trouble for Mom. Whether it be hosting a party for two hundred people at her home without help, visiting a sick friend in the hospital, or putting dinner on the table for the family each night, she managed it all seemingly with ease. This is more remarkable when you consider that her workday typically began at 4:00 a.m. and ended at 5:00 p.m., six days a week. On the seventh day, she rested. She seemed to always be attending to others' needs while dispatching her enormous personal and business responsibilities without complaint. She was absolutely amazing.

Mom's decorating business gave her a podium, and the nature of the work made her intimately involved with families of wealth and power. It turns out that a big decorating job can take months, and the clients often find it to be the most important thing going on in their lives at that time. Not only was Mom the decorator, she was also the peacemaker, advisor, psychiatrist, and family counselor, all rolled up into one. She wore her heart on her sleeve, and she loved to take charge. Many came to her with their most sensitive family matters, and she dove right in. They listened, they were thankful, and they were loyal. Her counsel was still in demand well after the jobs were completed, and she was always happy to help. Her following was huge. Unfortunately, as Mom's influence mushroomed, so did the number of lessons my sister and I were forced to endure.

Unlike other mothers who badgered their kids about school performance, our mother only looked at our report cards if we asked her to. Instead, she was concerned with entirely different things, like family, responsibility, creativity, and hard work. To Mom, being different was an aspiration that best described an authentic person rather than a person warranting concern. If you ever were impressed by anything acquired by money, you had to be prepared to hear, "If you like that sort of thing." And should you settle on choices considered more conventional, you would prepare for her most unflattering designation: "common." We were tasked to stay busy, and if she ever asked what we were doing, and we responded

"Just relaxing," we received the deadly "We don't relax in this family."

Mom loved the creative and always encouraged my involvement, despite my relentless efforts to resist. I will never forget when she approached me on the street, asking if I would like to take ballet lessons. I looked at her in disbelief. Not only did that offend every sensibility in my body, but it also showed her total lack of awareness of the environment in which I lived. I was struggling just to survive in the Westbury schools, and it was safe to say that if anyone overheard that gem, I would be a dead man. But she was unconcerned with how others saw things and wished I were capable of more independent thinking. Fitting in was a total cop-out.

As we got older, what was once a gentle prod soon became a blow from a sledgehammer. Mom was extremely disapproving of a culture she judged to be self-centered, overly indulgent, and lacking in resilience. It was her mission to do everything in her power to disabuse us of ever following this path. Consequently, we were apportioned very little space for emotional weakness. For her, this was a complete waste of time and energy, and was characteristic of a self-absorbed person. There were no deep conversations or shoulders to lean on. Instead, any trace of negative emotion was instantly cauterized, diminished and dispatched. Words were palliatives that undermined real therapy, which came from taking action and thus control.

In some respects, our allegiance to action served to dispatch certain emotional conventions that were common in other families. We didn't speak of love; it was understood. We shouldn't look to praise for validation; that was for others who were showy and self-indulgent. In fact, should we ever appear a bit too needy, my mother would instantly summon a story of someone whose circumstance was far more challenging and whose accomplishment far more meaningful. Westbury provided ample examples to reinforce our good fortune, and she left no quarter for sadness and disappointment.

I presume that it was a sense of guilt stemming from this constant barrage of emotional warfare that led me to develop my own brand of psychological offense against selfishness. Whenever I was feeling down, for whatever reason, I would think of people I knew who were less fortunate and call upon their circumstances to extinguish my mood. I was completely intolerant of weakness in myself, given my perception of our relatively good economic fortune, even though one could argue that our circumstances were actually quite modest.

I looked to my cousin Lois more than anyone else to serve in this capacity. Lois was a bit older than me, and when she was born, it was common practice to put premature infants in incubators shortly after birth. On occasion, hospitals applied too much oxygen when caring for newborn infants. This is how Lois, who was born with sight, had effectively been blind since birth.

During my youth, our families visited frequently, and Lois always sported an infectious smile. I never detected any bitterness or regret, just genuine warmth combined with a wonderful, empathetic spirit. She was always interested in others, and generous with praise and support. Her consistently joyful and optimistic disposition was inspiring and made a big impact on me.

Unfortunately, the message received was far askew from the message delivered. For some reason, at a very young age, I chose to put my own peculiar spin on things and used her example to develop a bit of an unyielding coping mechanism. When I had trouble with school, tests, a friend, petty jealousies—you name it—I would think of Lois and cast my problems in a very dim light. In fact, I would usually end up embarrassed that I allowed them to surface at all. This left very little room for self-pity, which was probably a good thing. But it also left little room for sadness and disappointment. This disposition required that I develop a mental toughness that quickly insulated me from acknowledging and exploring any negative thoughts or emotions. In the long run, it meant that I learned to bury the negative thoughts and feelings that are terribly unhealthy to leave unprocessed. I don't think that Lois would have approved at all.

In our family the message was always one of strength; weakness and vulnerability were never an option. This rigid disposition came with lasting mental and emotional consequences. The willingness and personal permission to be vulnerable is an important part of personal development. When a person is willing to be vulnerable, they are willing to relinquish control in search of answers and relationships beyond their reach. They are willing to accept personal risk in exchange for the prospect of reaching a place of greater meaning. They are willing to trust when fair compensation is unsure. *By making weakness unacceptable, vulnerability was not an option, and with vulnerability absent, trust was largely off the table.*

Although she spoke with great authority and conviction, understanding Mom and her mission was no simple task. It is fascinating that the same woman who tried to immunize her children from wasteful emotion in fact lived a life completely dictated by emotional obligation. Her empathy for her workers, clients, friends, and especially family was boundless, as was her willingness and energy to act and defend.

An interesting example of such behavior came when I confronted her about my cousin, who had stolen all my bar mitzvah money twenty years earlier. The revelation came after a conversation I had with Dad at a time when I was trying to learn more about the frequent home robberies we suffered during my youth. When sharing details about the three robberies, he casually mentioned that my cousin had committed one of them. He then shared that this was the same cousin who was responsible for stealing all the checks at my coming-of-age party.

I was not aware that my cousin had committed one of the robberies. And I certainly wasn't aware that he had stolen all my Bar Mitzvah money. I had handed all the checks I received directly to my parents, and they took care of the money. When I later asked Mom why she had never told me, she simply explained that my cousin had drug problems and that we had gotten most of the money back anyway. She wasn't angry. She didn't raise her voice to her relatives. She didn't care about the lost money. She was simply sad for the boy. And because none of us were evolved enough to respond in a fashion she deemed appropriate, none were granted access to the information. That was the way it was with so many of the tales of infirmity and sadness. These were her burdens to bear alone, and information was given out on a strictly need-to-know basis, and really, no one ever needed to know.

When information was of a personal nature, nothing ever got out. I think that if she were imprisoned in Guantanamo Bay, she wouldn't have broken. This drove my wife crazy when she first joined the family. In her family, even the smallest problems were worthy of an immediate family conference that could last for days. In my family, Mom could literally have a major-medical procedure and not share a single word with any of us. When, at a much later date, I might learn of a particular medical issue and inquire, her immediate response was always the same: "How would your knowing have helped?" Now, at her more advanced stage in life, when illness is more common and she sometimes requires assistance getting about, we laugh at her attempts to keep my sister and me in the dark.

Although her body is less able, her will to save the world from itself remains undiminished. She remains ready at a moment's notice to take action in any crisis and is hopeful that her example will motivate my sister and me to remain committed to this sacred work. In her eighties, even as infirmity has taken its toll, Mom is still willing to travel hours to all manner of events, both happy and sad, to show support for people whose relation is so obscure that it is hard to understand, even after careful explanation. And if we try to counsel a less draining course of action, we are vigorously shut down. She is the only one who truly knows what needs to be done and has the strength and willpower to follow through. We simply wouldn't understand. There is an extraordinary vanity one could ascribe to her relentless selflessness, but there is also a soul that few, if any, have the compassion plus endurance to match. Her actions clearly form the foundation of the charitable spirit that lies at the heart of my being.

Mom was different. She never worried about conventional things. She never cared about status or money. She loved to work, she loved to create, and she loved to help. She actually wanted me to attend a less demanding college where I would have more time to explore and experience life. In her opinion, responsibility would be a big part of my life soon enough, and there were more important things to do than simply keep your head buried in books. And when I told her I was quitting college in the middle of my sophomore year, it didn't bother her for a moment. Her philosophy was that no one was going to stop me from being who I was supposed to become. All I needed was a supportive family, hard work, a resilient attitude, and a good heart.

This was not your standard-issue Jewish Long Island mom. She was fiercely independent, fiercely liberal, fiercely unconventional, and fiercely protective of all those she loved. And all that went double for her relationship with Dad. They never fought. He wore clothes he bought at Sears, and she looked like she came out of *Vogue* magazine, and each thought the other was great exactly as he or she was. Because of her enormous popularity, they were constantly invited to elegant affairs, parties, and dinners, but they rarely went out. They were both exhausted from work, and their true happiness came from spending time with family. Nothing else really mattered all that much. And, to circle back to the original question at hand, I think these ultra-secure, independent, liberal, and strong people led me to choose Westbury schools over Jericho, and when I made that decision, they didn't blink.

HIGH SCHOOL

J unior high went by without incident, but high school was a whole new ball game. It started with the first days, known as Initiation Week. It was open season on all incoming tenth-graders. The older kids dragged the younger kids into the bathrooms and beat the shit out of them. On my first day, my neighbor saw me walk into school and immediately told me to turn around and walk home because the violence was out of control, and some kid was taken to the hospital.

I obediently followed instructions and didn't return for several days. I remember seeing Mom when I got home. I gave her the rundown and informed her that I planned to spend the first few days of school at home. She had no problem with my strategy. You see, she had once said to me that if she had been born Black, she would have been very violent because of the treatment Blacks suffered in this country. She saw these kids as victims lashing out in response to an immoral system, rather than as overly aggressive assholes looking to have some fun with the new kids. There was no sympathy on the home front; her philosophy was, "Just do what you need to do, stay safe, and get back to work."

As I got into the rhythm of high school, I learned to always keep my head on a swivel. The school was built on two square levels, so there were always two routes when changing classes; you chose the route based on who was in the hallway and what kind of activity was going on. Fights were constant. You could always sense the beehive of activity, voices, and characters when something was brewing, and it was best to stay clear. There were four adults whose sole jobs were to roam the hallways, trying to keep the violence in check, but peace was a commodity in rare supply. And, of course, you always had to stay vigilant when approaching any of the bathrooms that occupied the corners of the school because if you were pulled in, your prospects were grim. In fact, until my senior year, I regularly walked the mile home when I needed to go to the bathroom. Unfortunately, there were some places that you couldn't avoid, like the daily trip to the lunchroom, where you inevitably had the misfortune of being greeted by several thugs asking for money at the entrance. When you begged poverty, you always heard the same refrain before they patted you down: "Any money I find, I keep."

Although I went through school relatively un-scathed, there was one incident that really showed the risks involved. The cafeteria was next to the gym, and after I finished my lunch, I always went in to play basketball. If Westbury was mostly Black, the gym was all Black. And on one particular day, one of the real idiots in the school turned over a fire extinguisher in the corner of the gym. When the cafeteria aid arrived to escort him to the principal's office, he promptly told the aid to fuck off. After the aid left to gather reinforcements, the witch-hunt for the snitch was on. I would say there were about fifty kids in the gym that day playing about six different games, and when the search began to find the guilty party who had told the aid—big surprise—he decided it was the White guy. The next thing I saw was this six-foot-four-inch guy up in my grill, fist raised, shouting, "Admit it! You told!" while forty-nine Black guys stood behind him in a semicircle, all screaming, "Hit him!"

This is where the calculations kick in big-time. Who is he, who does he know, what is he carrying, and how far will he go? You see, if you choose to fight, you may win or lose, but actually, the more important question is "What happens next?" Should you win in the gym, in front of forty-nine other guys, it most certainly doesn't end there. So I decided to take the hit, and I closed my eyes at the moment of expected contact. When the blow failed to arrive, I opened my eyes and was stunned to see that, for some unknown reason, the coolest guy in the gym had grabbed the guy's arm and told him to leave me alone. I was saved that day, and he wouldn't even let me say thanks. But the larger point of the story was that my instincts were right. Later that week, the boy who threatened me hit another boy over the head with a lead pipe and put him in the hospital with real, long-term damage, and the kid I had faced was taken to jail.

There were certainly a lot of negative things associated with going to school in Westbury, but there were also some big positives. I did develop really sharp instincts that have enabled me to read people pretty damn fast, and on a deeper level, I got a ground-floor view of the unfairness that is suffered by people with disadvantages. Kids came to school hungry, and many needed free lunches to get fed. Education was often a secondary consideration to safety, and learning really suffered. Many were shipped off on buses each day to attend a special school for basic job training, rather than given extra resources to compensate for learning challenges that could have kept them in more conventional learning environments. Adding fuel to the fire, Westbury was surrounded by many affluent communities, providing vivid reminders of the differences between those with, and those who must do without. From this vantage point, I developed a deep sense of social justice and fairness that has always been at the core of all of my most important actions and decisions. I believe my mother was most approving of my educational tradeoffs.

Despite the somewhat challenging environment, I feel privileged to have grown up with wonderful friends, a caring family, a sense of freedom, and laughter, which were sources of infinite personal nourishment. But there was also plenty of heavy baggage that I was required to carry. At school it was imperative that I acquire a hard outer shell that gave off a vibe of strength and self-confidence. And at home, the marching orders were clear from the get-go: independence, strength, hard work, no regrets, no complaints, no vanity, no validation, and no displays. We were actually a Quaker family masquerading as New York Jews. The good stuff was all there; we just didn't waste time talking about it. It required a quiet, confident understanding, and I was okay with that.

And from this background—straddling security and violence, equality and inequality, lectures and levity—I developed a strong sense of duty, a real feeling of urgency and a willingness to do the work. Unfortunately, from this same background I also developed a posture that was not very approachable and a disposition that was not open to approach. *Trust was never going to be easy for me. I always knew that if I wanted to get things done, I had to do them myself.*

GROWTH

The academic education I received in Westbury was sorely lacking. In fact, in my graduating class of 320, I believe only twenty went on to four-year college programs. Despite this relatively uninspired educational environment, things changed quite radically after I decided to follow my mother's suggestion in the summer between eleventh and twelfth grades and enroll in the Cornell University summer educational program.

This experience was so extraordinarily different from all that I had known that it is hard to connect all the dots. This was my first exposure to college, and I found this place to be incredible. The facilities were amazing, the course catalogue overwhelming, the teachers inspiring, and, for some reason, it all conspired to create an excitement about learning I had never before imagined. After reading the course descriptions, I settled on something familiar and something not, biology and existentialism. Forget biology—existentialism completely blew my mind. It may be hard to picture, but before this, I had never voluntarily read a book nor been given a real academic writing assignment in school. Sure, we read textbooks and wrote short essays about the readings, but real, analytical writing assignments simply did not exist. So here I was, a nonreader, taking on Sartre, Camus, Flaubert, and Dostoevsky. I believe we read more than six books in six weeks, and they were intense.

I had a lot to overcome. I had absolutely no academic endurance, and I lacked virtually all of the skills and strategies needed to approach reading and writing assignments of this nature. Fortunately, the teacher was incredible. Prior to this class, the notion of finding anything about learning to be interesting or worthy of effort was completely alien to me. But this guy made me want to read, simply so that I could participate in the classroom discussions. Aided by his passionate and compelling analysis of the texts, I was actually beginning to think for the first time. I don't want to sound overly dramatic, but up until this point, school had very little to do with my life. It was relatively easy to do well with little to no effort, and that is exactly how much I applied. This was not a consequence of some exceptional ability I possessed but rather a function of a school and student body whose priorities were anything but academic. I had a long way to go, but for the first time, I saw what school could be and I really liked it.

The other really compelling part of the Cornell experience was the people. This was a chance to meet entirely new types of people from different places and, most importantly, with radically different priorities. These kids really valued education and were all about achievement. They studied hard and studied with purpose. They selected classes as part of well-conceived plans and had clear strategies to succeed. This was all new to me. They were approachable, interesting, and simply different from the kids in my school. And there were girls.

One of the less obvious liabilities of going to school in Westbury was that the girls were largely unavailable. There was no mixed-race dating, and the Italians were a very tight community who really kept to them selves, making the pool of available women brutally small. So I genuinely believe that this experience changed everything. Socially, I made a whole new group of friends who got me out of Westbury my senior year. I had my first meaningful experiences with women that were far too long in the making, and I began to see myself in a whole new way. I began to appreciate and value my abilities as a thinking person, and with that, my expectations and horizons changed forever.

My next stop was Northwestern University. Although Cornell did whet my appetite for higher education, my personal product was a long way from finished. Let's start with the application process. After monumental struggles with the English portions of the standardized exams, I eventually managed some decent scores and started scouring the college guides for places to go. There was no visiting and little counseling, just a book and my general impressions. The students at Cornell certainly instilled in me a desire to go to an academic institution, but how would I choose?

I knew that Westbury afforded me certain advantages in the selection process, so I had a chance to attend a school far above my high school accomplishments. I remember wanting to leave the East Coast, but I understood that we could not afford the flights to the West Coast. There was no way I was going to the South, as I assumed that Southerners were deeply prejudiced. The Ivy League sounded out of my league, and I wanted to be in a somewhat urban environment, which I thought would be more familiar. When all was processed, Chicago sounded just right. When I read that the University of Chicago was in a tough neighborhood, I decided that I had paid my dues on that score and applied for an early decision to beautiful, suburban Northwestern University.

With all of my thoughtful plotting and planning, you might assume that I agonized over the application to get everything just right. I did, too, until I received my acceptance letter from the engineering school. I thought that I had applied to the College of Arts and Sciences, so when I got the letter, I freaked out and called the university. Yes, they confirmed, I had checked the box for the School of Engineering. And although I didn't know what engineering was, they assured me that I could transfer soon after I started. Clearly, I had a long way to go before this academic jewel was well polished.

University life was challenging right from the start. This was the beginning of my new life as an adult, and I felt there was no place for any parental interference. So when it came time to travel to Chicago, I chose to go on my own, accompanied only by my ninety pounds of luggage. I was equal parts nervous and excited. I could not wait to start my new life, but I had never traveled on my own, never been to Chicago and didn't know anyone at the school. There was a free Northwestern bus scheduled to leave O'Hare Airport at 3:00 p.m., and I arrived at the location with plenty of time to spare. Unfortunately, the bus was not so punctual, arriving after 6:00.

As you might guess, my enthusiasm for the day was a bit misplaced at this point. By the time we arrived on campus, all the welcome wagons were long gone. To make matters worse, everyone on the bus lived on south campus, except me and one other guy, who lived up north. When the bus driver asked if he could leave us in between our two dorms, suggesting that they were very close, we both willingly agreed. That is when I discovered that I had to carry my luggage over a quarter of a mile in temperatures that were still registering in the high eighties.

When I finally got to the dorm (shirt off, profusely sweating, sporting a frustration-inspired touch of rage), you can imagine the sight my new roommate spied when I poked my head in the room and barked my first greeting; "Help me bring my shit upstairs!" If I had only taken a moment to notice his parents sitting on the opposite side of the room, I might have summoned up a bit of common courtesy, or so I like to think. He helped me with my stuff, I politely introduced myself, and he didn't return for several days. In Westbury, aggression was the go-to posture; a quick temper was an asset and physical response was a very normal reaction. Unfortunately, none of these qualities served any greater purpose in educated society. I had a lot of work in front of me before I could find my place among my new peers.

In addition to this high-quality introduction, there was apparently a backstory that I was unaware of at the time. All incoming freshman had to submit a picture and declare their intended major for inclusion in the freshmen handbook that was distributed prior to our arrival at school. Being a bit tone-deaf to the notion of first impressions, I had taken my photo in an old-fashioned photo booth after wrestling practice and, from some magical place of make-believe, I chose to declare my major to be urban planning. I guess I looked and described myself as being straight out of the ghetto.

Apparently, after receiving the freshmen book, my future roommate had already petitioned vigorously for a roommate change that had been denied by the university. After he met the real thing, I assume that he was making his best attempt to transfer to a new school entirely, and who could possibly blame him? After living with his cousin in Skokie for a few days, he returned to the dorm, and I was so glad he did. After a bit of effort, we became great friends and remain close to this day.

Thus alone, following said meeting with my roommate, I ventured out for my first evening on campus, following the sounds of music to an area of large, old, stone houses adjacent to my dorm. There was clearly partying going on everywhere, and I cautiously staked out a spot on a large, empty patio of one of the houses where everyone seemed to be having a great time inside. All of a sudden, the music stopped, and the guys inside started screaming and yelling as they came charging outside onto the patio, where I alone was standing. My well-developed instincts kicked in, and I took off like a rocket. When I reached a safe distance, I looked back to see a large group of guys surrounding one kid in particular, while they all jumped and screamed something unfamiliar. I didn't know it, but this fraternity had just gotten a new pledge. More importantly, I had never heard the terms "fraternity" or "pledge." I just knew that I had no people, and this looked risky.

As I managed many of the initial tests and began to make some friends in the dorm, I began to face the challenges of academic life. Cornell had been wonderful and had exposed me to really talented students, but academic performance was not yet a high priority. Now, achievement was measured by fiercely sought-after grades, and the engineering college was a particularly demanding school at the university. The students were certainly smart, but more importantly, they arrived much better prepared, having come from competitive high schools. In addition, the engineering school was organized to be a particularly difficult test. Grades were issued on a strict curve: 10 percent As, 30 percent Bs, 30 percent Cs, and then the rest. And there were no pluses or minuses. The first stop after A was B, and so on. So, basically, only two-thirds of the students were going to survive, and only about 40 percent were going to experience some measure of success, and I was starting with two arms tied firmly behind my back.

The first year and a half was a real struggle. A steady diet of Bs and Cs really sapped my spirit. I remember talking to my roommate about quitting school. I distinctly recall a particular conversation in which I spoke of my hard work and lack of results, and his immediate response was laughter. This was a risky move, given my incredibly thin skin and explosive temper. But before I could respond to this insult, he was quick to explain that I was doing nothing, only studying about thirty to forty minutes a night, when all the rest of them were clocking two to four hours of study time each day. I really couldn't wrap my head around that. I had not noticed how much everyone studied. How could I possibly do more?

Even though I had made some friends, I kept a pretty effective barrier between my fragile ego and the rest of the student body. So, although I was in the community, I was still a bit isolated. I was aware that I was different, but I failed to comprehend the scope of the difference. Further testimony to this fact came when, at this largely white university, a member of the Black fraternity invited me to rush. I kindly declined. I clearly held the Westbury in me as a badge of honor, not because I was so proud of it, but because I felt it was something I could claim as different. Deep down, I was fearful that I couldn't compete academically. This translated into the distinct vibe of a guy with a real attitude problem, an assessment shared by none other than the two Black, drug-dealing football players from Philadelphia who lived across the hall.

Evidence of the general feeling I evoked was abundantly clear when my birthday arrived in December of my sophomore year. We had a seldom-used tradition in the dorm of stripping guys naked and throwing them in Lake Michigan for their birthdays, but common sense generally prevailed as the temperatures took a dive in the winter. No such restraint was called for when it came to my birthday. My roommate began placing banners all over the dorm and cafeteria for weeks in advance announcing for all to come and join in the "lake-ing of Lewin."

At first, it was a cute joke, but as the day approached, the enthusiasm began to build, and as the temperatures continued to drop, I started getting pretty scared. When the fateful day arrived, about two hundred kids assembled to join in the celebration. Although I put up a valiant effort to evade the hoards, they eventually overwhelmed me. I was then hoisted in the air and taken to the lake in my birthday suit. I remember that the lake was particularly frozen that year, so after wandering a bit in search of water, they ended up leaving me out there on the ice as they marched back to the dorm in celebration. Thank God a few of the more compassionate revelers brought a blanket and escorted me back to the dorm to infuse some alcohol into my damaged and shivering body.

Maybe I had become overly invested in our family's fondness for being different. Everyone sure knew I was different and I can't claim it was working to my advantage thus far. But the real coming-to-Jesus moment occurred prior to the "lake-ing," during my sophomore year. That is when I called my mother to inform her of my decision to not return to college following the Christmas break. You see, in addition to many other sacrifices, my mom had pawned her wedding ring to help finance my college education, and I was of the opinion that Bs and Cs were not worthy of the price of tuition. As you might imagine, Mom had little to say beyond "Fine." Before returning home, I scheduled a road trip for the Thanksgiving holiday to the University of Michigan to spend time with a friend who had graduated from Northwestern after my freshman year and had entered Michigan's prestigious clinical psychology program. My friend was a Black guy who had grown up in downtown Chicago and loved the city for its sophisticated arts and dining pleasures. Now, he found himself in Ann Arbor, Michigan, a town where the biggest cultural activity was football (something my friend hated) and in a program that was scheduled for five years, but (he soon found out) few graduated in less than seven years.

Now you know why he invited me for a visit. We were sharing the same grim outlook regarding our respective circumstances. One of the amazing statistics

41

he shared with me was that over ten thousand people had applied for admittance to his program, and only eleven were ultimately enrolled. Although this impressive ratio suggested accomplishment and prestige, after closer inspection following my arrival, it was obvious that the highly selective nature of the program also served to collect an incredibly bizarre group of highly driven yet confused souls. Even though I had never taken a psychology course, when the first student I met was a woman sporting a bronze belt buckle that was about six inches in diameter, I had no problem cracking the code.

Overall, the group had a frenetic, obsessive feel to it, and most seemed to feel trapped in their circumstances. The Oscar Wilde quote comes to mind: "There are only two tragedies in life: one is not getting what one wants, and the other is getting it." These students all got into this exclusive program and were now dealing with it, for better or worse, and my friend was feeling backed into a corner as he contemplated the merits of his graduate school decision. We both felt that we had made mistakes and were not up to the challenges. Fortunately, we had reached this moment at the same time and were both anxious to find help.

We talked endlessly and processed as much of the rational and irrational as we could digest before needing a break. To relax and change our focus, we decided to take in a new movie called "Oh, God!" starring George

Burns as God. It was a really funny film, but it was also deceptively thoughtful, with an underlying message of faith—faith in things extraordinary and faith in one-self. For whatever reason, it resonated, and combined with our long weekend of endless conversations, we both resolved to give our programs a bit more time.

This was a really unusual circumstance for me. Before this visit I don't ever recall actively seeking out a friend or advisor for help. This trip provided me with the distance from my peers that I needed so that I could feel safe admitting weakness and exploring failure. And it was the first time that I ever remember being totally honest about my feelings with someone else. The experience was incredibly helpful, but at the time I don't think I fully appreciated what I had been willing to do and all that had been accomplished.

My first steps back following Christmas break were initially met with disappointment, but my new resolve was not easily derailed, and success was soon to follow. As I described earlier, I was not only poorly prepared but I also had little awareness of the strategies needed to succeed.

Unfortunately, it was now time to take one of the weed-out classes in engineering: Statistics I. There were about 130 kids in the class, and I managed a C with a thirteen on the final exam—the advantage of a strict, curved grading system. That was certainly deflating, but the big change came the following semester, in Statistics

II. The curriculum suggested that you take one after the other, so I was completely surprised when I walked into the classroom on the first day of class to find only thirteen students in attendance. Needless to say, these likely were the kids who got As in Statistics I and, as was so often the case in the engineering school, none were from this country.

Despite the long odds, I bit the bullet and decided to take my medicine. Magically, something changed. Things started making sense, and the investment needed to digest new concepts eased. Somehow, I got an A. There were probably only two distributed, and I got one of them, competing with the best of the best.

Putting all the pieces together to explain my academic rags-to-riches story is not so easy. I would like to assign attribution to something specific, but I think it was more likely a function of greater acclimation to this new environment, an increase in stamina for studying, a greater level of maturity and, most importantly, my competitive need to succeed. I was always a good student of competition and was quick to adapt. As my failures piled up, I began to pay attention to how my fellow students studied. The first thing I recall noticing was the way they prioritized their energy. All effort was focused on planning and plotting for test taking. The acquisition of subject matter knowledge was not the prime focus of attention; rather, it was a byproduct on the road to good grades. Thus, in-class attention and subsequent review was largely devoted to predicting what was going to appear on the next exam rather than academic exploration and curiosity.

Up to this point, I had never really understood the difference between learning and test taking, and never treated them differently. Classroom learning and the study that followed had comprised somewhat of a random walk, as I wandered through the requirements and dwelled on those things I found most interesting. But now I began to study my teachers, and I invested time and energy to anticipate their direction. For some reason, I was good at it. Maybe this was the upside of Westbury, where reading people was a very useful skill. Suddenly, tests presented fewer surprises, and my study time became infinitely more efficient. From then on, my grades soared—mostly As, with some Bs—and I never looked back. The love for learning that I first tasted at Cornell was back, and school changed forever. As my successes grew, so did my self-esteem. With that, my social life blossomed, education was a joy, and I had much more time to simply explore.

One of the first new things I did was join the Northwestern crisis hotline. It was a wonderful project that provided telephonic crisis counseling to those in the Chicago area who were experiencing critical moments of indecision from midnight to 6:00 a.m. We had to take classes to learn how to talk with people in moments of desperation, assess the priorities of their situations, and move them to local resources that could be of immediate assistance. The calls were draining, but the sense of satisfaction gained from connecting with someone in need was an important new feeling.

This was the first time that I had fundamentally chosen to shift my attention to others versus focusing exclusively on myself. In my early years, I was sort of thrust into being concerned for others because of my mother's activism and the dynamics of racial politics in Westbury. But there is a big difference between following the agenda of another and forging a path of your own. This time, my involvement was personal rather than circumstantial. Consciously, I began to feel a sense of purpose that previously had been beyond my appreciation.

I graduated Westbury street-smart and physically capable, and now my college experience allowed me to begin to evolve as a thinking person. My academic success at Northwestern was an incredible personal accomplishment. I was completely unprepared, completely on my own, yet I figured out how to succeed in a highly competitive academic environment. For a very long time, I had been unsure any of this was possible.

Now, for the first time, I was willing and able to engage with a much broader group of people, with a sense of confidence and intellectual belonging.

Don't get me wrong: I graduated Northwestern far from a finished product. Most of the work I did at Northwestern was math and science oriented. When combined with my beginnings in Westbury, I would confidently argue that I still completely lacked the well-rounded background of an educated man. These gaps were very clear to me and constantly kept me on my heels when I was around educated people, but I was pretty good at covering up my deficits as I tried to assemble the missing pieces.

As I look back, life at Northwestern was wonderful, and many of my friendships continue strong to this day. A group of five of us still try to go to one football game each year with as many family members as we can bring, and each week during the season, we are all texting feverishly during game time, with our own brands of bias and enthusiasm. The education was absolutely first-rate, and the exposure to such a broad mix of students from across the country and the world was culturally invaluable. And I am happy to say that both of my children attended wonderful summer programs at the university, and my daughter enrolled as a freshman forty years after I first arrived on campus.

But, along with all the personal growth I experienced during my time at the university, there existed a prevailing societal attitude of malaise and loss. Growing up in the 1960s and early 1970s, I had the feeling that the camera's lens had moved beyond the post–World

War II period of patriotic pride and economic revival, and had shifted its focus onto the pressing matters of social change and justice. The country was polarized, the images of conflict were vivid and terrifying, and the leaders were charismatic. People were fighting for things that they really cared about and were willing to pay the price of involvement. The music was rich, drugs were everywhere, and social activism was part of the fabric of life. Growing up in Westbury during this period gave me a wonderful vantage point to observe, learn, and participate.

But the deaths of Martin Luther King, Jr., John F. Kennedy, and Bobby Kennedy, the ending of our involvement in Vietnam, and the closing of the Watergate trials seemed to suck the air out of the country's collective sails. Far less had changed than people had hoped, and institutions of all kinds were no longer to be trusted. The long period of "we" had devolved into the period of "me," and social causes were replaced by cynicism and personal gain. The country was experiencing a period of great change, and the feeling was palpable.

As a result, protest marches and rallies for causes were nonexistent during my college years, and there was little attachment to things greater than self-interest. Thus, a sense of school spirit and greater purpose were sorely lacking, fostering a stronger attachment to the credentials awarded than the richness of the experience and the lasting worth of affiliation with a formidable place of growth and development. This was a product of the times, not the place, but it did little to change my obsessive self-reliance, my reluctance to engage with others and my difficulty offering another my trust, all of which might have benefitted from a more collegial and cooperative atmosphere.

Following graduation from college in 1979, I moved back to New York City. After a brief stay at IBM, I joined Wall Street at the beginning of the bull market in 1982. And as I already indicated, my mindset and personal values were not in sync with the prevailing norms of the times or the heady times yet to come. Maybe you recall the famous line from Oliver Stone's movie *Wall Street* that "Greed is good." This was the beginning of the period when greed was considered good for our country's economy. And for the next several decades, the financial markets were at the center of our national economic identity. The power players on Wall Street were referred to as "Masters of the Universe," and boastfulness and displays of wealth were very much part of the fashion of the times and the culture.

Despite this climate, my cultural compass was firmly rooted in Westbury and my values still reflected those first learned from my family. More broadly speaking, the "me" ethic of the 1980s was very much in conflict with the selflessness ethic preached at home. And although our allegiance to our family values was a bit excessive, in the case of selflessness I was completely onboard. Fitting in and offering my trust in this environment was never going to be easy. Although I worked in the mainstream, my mindset was unorthodox, and this proved to be a source of constant difficulty.

WORK

F or all the progress I made in college, the workplace
once again exposed the fact (with little ambiguity)
that I still had a long way to go. My first job was with
IBM. This was when IBM was still at its zenith in the
late 1970s. They employed over 350,000 people and had
revenues in excess of most countries' GDP. I think it is
fair to describe it at the time as our most valued corporate citizen. IBM was a cultural icon of the business
community and a symbol of national pride. "Big Blue"
represented a lot of things, one of which was a standard
of business comportment. Everyone knew the drill: blue
pinstripe suit, white shirt, black wingtip shoes, and either a red or yellow tie. They defined the corporate

uniform of the day and, with it, a prescription for behavior that was well understood, well respected, and followed without exception.

There apparently was one family that didn't get the memo. I had an internship at one of the IBM plants the summer between my junior and senior years in college and did well helping with the design of a new type of electronic display, so I had a little edge in the post college interview process. But life in the plants was more informal, and the dress code really only applied to the front-line guys who interfaced with customers, whether they were salesmen or engineers. So when it was time to interview for one of these hard-to-acquire, customer-facing positions, I'm not sure that I was armed with all the necessary information needed to purchase the appropriate business attire.

To further compound my error, I chose to enlist the services of my mother to help make this mission-critical purchase. You should understand that this is the same lady who tried to dress me in a Nehru jacket for my bar mitzvah. Anyway, off we went to the discount department store to find the perfect outfit. Between the two of us we came up with a black sports jacket and two pairs of tan pants that I could rotate through the week when I began my job. We really nailed that choice for the IBM interview or, for that matter, any of my engineering and consulting interviews. Add to that my beard and long hair, and to all others, I must have looked like a shoo-in for unemployment.

In spite of my attire, I made it through the initial rounds of interviews before I was sent to New York for my final interview. This was another eye-opener. I sat across the desk from an elegant, six-foot-four, Harvard-educated, World War II fighter pilot who was the poster boy for all that I was not. Whatever it said in my file must have largely decided that I should be hired because I think this guy was surprised to see me sitting across from him. I should have been disposed of long before I reached his desk. But he did have one volley he could throw at me to see if he could change the outcome. Amazingly, I handled it well beyond my maturity level.

By this point in the job-search process, I had actually gotten a few job offers in the Chicago area. They generally were paying $16,000 to $18,000 per year to start. But I desperately wanted to come back to New York, and this job was right in the heart of Manhattan. You must understand that, as with all things IBM, starting salaries were not negotiable. A starting salary in the New York in the sales office was $12,700, with multiple raises to be given in the first year, based on performance. Everyone knew this, even I knew this, and certainly my Harvard-educated future boss knew this as well. So when he casually suggested at the end of the interview that he was prepared to offer me a position with a starting salary of about $10,000, amazingly, I didn't take the bait. I calmly accepted and later received my $12,700 starting salary, just like the thousands of other new hires that same summer.

IBM was a great place to work. There were tons of young people, and we traveled frequently for education in the first year as part of our training. This was all part of a carefully crafted plan to nurture, and more importantly acculturate, everyone into the IBM system. And one of the ways they did this was by sending us to Dallas, Texas every other month for thirty days of course work. This was academic work just like college, with the addition of one important factor: you were also graded on how you dressed. This was very serious stuff. Your raises were directly affected by your performance in school, so everyone was very focused. And magically, still sporting my unique brand of business attire, I was never penalized by the teachers. I knew guys who got marked down for wearing striped shirts, yet for some reason, I was left alone, and my raises never suffered.

Many months later, this whole wardrobe thing reared its head back in New York when my immediate boss called me in for a talk. I was working in an office of about five hundred employees, each of whom wore almost the exact same thing every day. So, when my boss started our session, he was somewhat at a loss for words. No one who worked for IBM ever needed to have this discussion. I remember clearly that he rubbed his face incessantly, desperately searching for a way to start. Painstakingly, he suggested that I possibly look around at how the other guys were dressing and maybe…. And that's when I stopped him. A light went off in my head, and I looked him straight in the eye and told him, "I got it. I will fix the problem immediately. Don't worry about a thing."

Once again, I enlisted my mother, and off we went to the discount store, in search of some new duds. Unfortunately, I had not fully grasped the entire scope of the problem. I thought my boss wanted me to get a suit. I didn't realize that it was supposed to be the IBM blue pin-stripped suit. So when I came to work over the next few days in my new green and-rust colored suits, everyone decided that this was a great victory for the office, and no one said another word about it.

I've thought long and hard about this story. It seems unimaginable that I did not notice that I was the only person in such a large office that dressed differently. It seems equally unimaginable that no one in my family could offer advice to steer me in the right direction. But it did happen, and upon reflection several observations come to mind.

One aspect of my behavior could have been attributed to my lack of awareness and first job naivety. Another aspect could have been linked to my unusual upbringing that taught me not to value superficial things like appearances. We were supposed to focus on what was considered to be the important stuff. But there may have been a third aspect of my behavior that could have been characterized as extreme arrogance. Being different was always highly valued in my family and yet here I was, at the company that valued conformity above all else. Whether it was a conscious or subconscious decision, I may have wanted to prove a point. Rather than make the easy concession and let my work speak for itself, I may have wanted to show that I could perform *and do it my way.*

I suspect the truth is some combination of all three of these statements. Quite frankly, I have no recollection of noticing how the others dressed nor do I recall others noticing how I dressed prior to the meeting with my boss. But if there is any shred of truth in the last statement, then I believe I may have possessed a level of self confidence that was completely unwarranted and an arrogance that would have made connection, accommodation, and trust very difficult to offer.

Despite my admiration for the company, after a short period of time I knew that it was not the place for me. I found the scale of the organization very intimidating and realized that culturally I was probably not the best fit for any meaningful advancement. So I took action immediately, and with IBM's financial support, I entered the evening program at NYU's graduate school of business. I actually finished this four-year program in just two years because I was so anxious to find a job that made sense. Life was pretty simple for the next two years: I worked 8:00 a.m. to 5:00 p.m., went to school from 6:00 p.m. to 10:00 p.m., and studied until I was exhausted. I did this year round for the next two years. It was a real bear, but I made it and graduated with strong grades and a master's degree in finance.

As I approached my last days in the MBA program, I did not have a clear vision of what I wanted to do. Fortunately, at NYU you were required to keep a résumé on file during your final year. One day I got a call from a recruiter, asking if we could meet. As soon as I walked into his office I knew that something was different. It was enormous and decorated with things that exuded power and influence: incredible furniture, plush rugs, and real art on the walls. It was my first time feeling that I was in the presence of someone with real power, and my instincts were not misplaced.

He explained that his client was looking for someone with a financial education and a background in technology, so I clearly fit the bill. After a reasonably thorough interview, he walked me through an explanation of the job. At this point, I was only vaguely aware of the whole Wall Street thing and certainly knew nothing about stocks and bonds. That apparently was not a big concern. They were more interested in a person with the right raw skills. After they completed their interview process and confirmed my interest, they assured me that the job was mine. Really—they could just say that, and it would happen? Well, they said it, and it happened. After a few perfunctory interviews with Merrill Lynch, I was offered a job as a technology analyst making $26,000 a year. I thought I was rich.

WALL STREET

Although I had taken a step in the right down sizing direction by leaving IBM and joining Merrill, I was still part of an enormous machine with over forty thousand employees. I remember getting that message loud and clear on my first day when I entered a crowded elevator to go to lunch. My boss reached over to introduce me to a large, imposing man on my left. He greeted me kindly, so I responded naively, "What do you do?" He responded, "I run this place." After the laughter died down in the elevator, I realized that although I had already interviewed in offices larger than my apartment, there was always someone with a bigger office, so

I needed to keep a low profile until all the information was in.

While it was abundantly clear that I was merely a small cog in this really big wheel, my role had become far more visible, and along with the visibility came the risks. I was a technology analyst, responsible for helping a senior analyst analyze and recommend the buying and selling of the largest tech companies in the world, including IBM, to the thousands of Merrill stockbrokers and customers. At the time, every person with money-management responsibility had to have an investment opinion about IBM. Its importance in the marketplace was far too big to ignore, so we were always in demand.

I recall one business trip when I flew to Dallas in the morning for a client breakfast, flew to San Antonio for lunch, and flew to Houston for dinner, before returning home at day's end. We were constantly on call for private meetings with managers in charge of billions of dollars of customer capital, and each morning, over the internal Merrill Lynch broadcast system, we were called upon to advise our massive brokerage system of our company's prospects and news of the day. With huge sums of money on the line, you could really feel the pressure. This was also the first time that I was around people competing for really big salaries and bonuses, numbers that were completely alien to me.

Thus, mistakes were very costly, and people pushed exceedingly hard to win.

Unfortunately for me, in addition to already being in a high-pressure environment, my boss was known to be particularly volatile with a wicked temper. He seemed to go through a new assistant every year or two. I'm sure that his expectations for me were no different. As it turned out, I spent the next couple of years nursing a pretty consistent case of stomach cramps. I remember one incident quite clearly, which accurately captured the pressure involved with working for my boss. One day he stormed into my office screaming, "Where are my glasses? Where are my glasses?" He started opening and closing my drawers, and I assumed that, if for some reason, they were found in my office, I was done. I immediately panicked and started looking everywhere as fast as I could, hoping to defuse this latest crisis.

It's interesting how pressure and tension can conspire to impair your faculties because his glasses were propped squarely on the top of his head, but I couldn't see them. You might find it particularly interesting to know that he was as bald as a cue ball.

This job was hard enough without the extra burden of a tightly wound boss. I did manage to spend two years there, longer than most of my predecessors. And although my stomach was tied tightly in a knot, I did learn a lot and accomplished some significant things. A highlight was writing and publishing the first Wall Street equity-research report on the subject of local area networking. This was part of the architecture that eventually evolved into what we now understand to be the Internet. The Internet became part of the public conversation after Netscape went public in 1995.

This report created a lot of visibility and helped me collect a number of attractive job offers at some of Wall Street's best firms. As an analyst at Merrill Lynch, my job was to help professional money managers invest their clients' capital. Now I wanted to be one of those professional managers. I wanted more freedom, more responsibility and more risk. I wanted to be tested and measured. I wanted to compete and I wanted to win. And although I was fortified by some initial successes, I still was not fully aware of how poorly equipped I was for the personal and professional hurdles yet to come.

MY SIDE JOB

Although work dominated my life and served as an important component of my development, there was an equally important parallel existence that consumed almost all of my spare time. Having grown up among those with great needs and disadvantages, I felt an overwhelming obligation to give back after receiving my first paycheck. When I wasn't working, exercising, or looking for women, I was involved in charity. I was actively engaged in volunteering with the Special Olympics, participating in tutoring and mentoring programs, working with crisis lines and help centers, and coaching basketball. I dedicated time weekly and never refused a request. This led to some extraordinary experiences.

One such experience came at a Lower East Side community center, where I volunteered as a math and reading tutor. As was always the case at these centers, the people were wonderful but completely lacking in the resources necessary to meet their needs. So it was no surprise when the head of the center asked me if I would also be willing to coach their basketball team. When I asked why she had asked me, her logic was quite simple: "You're tall. Maybe you know how to play?"

The task, however, was far from simple. This was a pretty well known basketball league that produced kids at big-time NCAA programs as well as the Junior Olympics, and even a few pros. Two salient facts about our community center are worth knowing. First, we were the only one located outside of Harlem. Second, we were the only one that was primarily Spanish rather than Black. This was important because our population was much more baseball- versus basketball-centric. As a result, fielding a team of interested and capable players to remotely compete in this league was a tall order.

After a healthy number of practices, we were ready for our first game. The first hurdle came when we all met at the center before leaving for the game, and some of our players arrived without uniforms. This was a big deal in the league because part of the experience included learning discipline and responsibility. For example, as a coach, I was required to wear a jacket and tie to the games to reinforce my image as a role model. So, when our center director chose to sit those without uniforms, given our thin margin for error, I assured her that it wouldn't happen again, and I would buy them the appropriate gear at a store near the game. This led to a pretty hysterical scene consisting of me chasing a dozen thirteen-year-old Spanish kids around a Harlem Kmart as game time grew near.

Before we get to the gym, let me set the scene. This was the very early 1980s, and New York was a shadow of its current self. Things were dangerous. Even my kids were on edge, many going uptown for the first time. I distinctly recall a lovely Black woman sitting as I stood on the ride uptown on the subway. At each stop above 86th Street, she would tug on my jacket, asking if I would consider getting off at the next stop. I guess that Friday night in Harlem was not for white guys wearing sports jackets. When we finally found our way to the gym, we were stunned. Far different than downtown, this was obviously the Friday-night entertainment for the entire housing project.

The first thing we noticed was the heat. It felt like the temperature was about ninety degrees on this cold, fall night. The next thing we saw was the opposing team, in their fast-moving layup line dressed in these incredible, gold-trimmed basketball outfits. And last—but far from least—were the gigantic speakers consuming the four corners of the gym, blasting music as everyone in the packed stands stood, dancing and singing to the beat. And because we were late, as soon as we entered the gym, the refs screamed, "Game on!"

Cut to the final scene. With three minutes to play, we were down sixteen points. I called time-out and rallied the troops. And with five seconds to go, we were down by one point, and we had the ball. Unfortunately, unlike the movies, we missed the last shot, but it was what followed that stayed with me. It was around 11:00 p.m. when we finished, and the place was filled with emotion. Quite frankly, I was a little nervous about getting to the subway and home safely, but in fact we could not have been greeted more warmly, with sincere handshakes and gestures of congratulations and admiration. They really loved the heart of our team and my willingness to come to their gym and compete. That old saying about books and their covers could never have been more accurate. But it seems that I needed to be smacked over thc head a few more times before this thoughtful adage actually began to sink in. These people could not have been nicer, and remember—this was when times were distinctly not nicer.

Another experience I remember fondly was working with a group of Special Olympians as both a coach and a chaperone for a basketball-tournament weekend in upstate New York. This was a ton of responsibility and an equal dose of work. But when we won a game by a score of four to three, the rewards far exceeded all the efforts expended. The crying and laughter expressed by all the players and coaches were images and feelings that will never be forgotten.

These and many other experiences in the charitable world made my life so much richer and laid the foundation for some of my greatest experiences yet to come. But, as with many things, there can be unforeseen costs. I was spending several hours each week on my charitable activities, and my attachment to the work and to the people I served ran extremely deep. As I helped them navigate some unimaginably difficult circumstances, it became more and more difficult for me to tolerate any form of sadness or self-pity, thereby reinforcing an unhealthy habit from childhood. And although charitable experiences did offer feelings of satisfaction, they also added fuel to my sense of personal responsibility, requiring increasing investments of time and energy. I was consumed with being an agent of change for those in need, and never allowed myself the time to consider that the agent may have needed some changing as well.

GOOD FORTUNE

My next place of employment after Merrill Lynch put me in proximity to people of real authority and accomplishment on Wall Street. Doors began to open to people and places that I formerly had been unaware even existed. This was the world of Harvard, Yale and Princeton, and of money like you can't believe. Although this was a new and completely alien world, I dove into the deep end with an unwarranted confidence that suggested I belonged.

My job was at an institution of great prestige, and this was still the old Wall Street where youth was not an asset but a liability of experience. I knew that I was willing to do the work necessary to succeed, but I had to figure out a way to acquire the experiences required to infuse the work with wisdom. In this latest place of business, there were roughly five hundred employees, of which about one hundred were considered investment professionals. Approximately fifty of them had achieved the coveted title of "partner," which enabled them to share in the firm's generous profit streams. The partners generally ranged in age from fifty to eighty-five years old. Of the remaining fifty investment professionals, I was one of the three youngest, at the age of twenty-six. This was no playground. This was a place for people of accomplishment who came to make money and finish their careers among true peers. It was also crystal clear to me that this was a place where I could fulfill my career aspirations, a place where I could measure myself against the best.

With this understanding, I launched myself on a path to compensate for my lack of experience by investing as much time as possible learning about the professional lives of the partners, soaking up every story and lesson from their decades of experience in the stock market. I did this for the next ten years, and it meaningfully changed my perspective and my understanding of how markets worked. In their offices and over meals, I grabbed every moment possible to pick their brains. I absorbed all they had to offer, and to further my education, they introduced me to their peers. In addition to these sources of knowledge, I constructed a business that allowed me to do analytical work for some of the great figures on Wall Street outside the firm. This gave me the chance to learn from some of the undisputed legends of money management. They let me get close, and my growth as an investor blossomed. My education was extraordinary.

As I acclimated to this new environment, I began to gain a vision of how my life could change. Boundaries were no longer fixed and I was anxious to test my limits. For the very first time, I sensed that my peculiar background afforded me certain advantages. Sure, I was new to this world of privilege and power, but I also possessed a balance of strengths that were more than worthy compensation. First learned in my earliest days in Westbury, my ability to read people and situations was outstanding. And my willingness to accommodate peculiar points of view was unique in a world that outwardly advocated risk taking but, in practice, was incredibly reluctant to drift from the status quo. This agility enabled a wide berth for alliances with professionals of great intellectual adventure and fertile ground to process and advance ideas of my own design. As my ideas gained audience, my confidence grew, and my prospects gathered momentum.

In August of 1987, I got the chance to manage a small pension fund for a generic-drug manufacturer. This was a tremendous opportunity to apply the skills I was beginning to develop. However, my stock-selection ambitions for the fund were slightly derailed by a stock market that was moving up smartly. Because of my reluctance to chase stocks moving up in price, I was only able to spend about 65 percent of the investable dollars.

As a matter of overview, I was trained as a stock picker; I processed one idea at a time, each on its own merits. Additionally, I had also gained some insight into how markets worked. One of the principle risks I was advised to guard against was the risk of rising interest rates. And in this particular market, interest rates were rising as quickly as stock prices. So I decided to take my first risk as a money manager and began to liquidate the portfolio as my holdings appreciated. As stocks and rates began to accelerate on the upside, so did my selling. As a result, on the day before the crash of October 1987, I was down to one position with some nice gains in the bank. If the market had continued rising, I would have been in real trouble with my first account, and my reputation in the firm would have been damaged. But I stayed with my disciplines. I was willing to be held accountable for my decision and I was unafraid to be different from almost all of my peers. On that next extraordinary trading day, everything changed.

The scene was incredibly eerie. I worked in a small trading room with about fifteen other investors, surrounded by dozens of private offices. The most noteworthy thing about Black Monday was the silence. In an environment known for volume, no one said a word, and not a single phone rang from the market's open until after trading closed. I don't even recall anyone getting up to go to the bathroom. Some of the people who worked in offices began to migrate into the trading room, and each simply sat down to join the silence. In our office, people were really committed to investing their own money as well as their clients' capital, and many were losing 20 to 30 percent of their personal net worth in a single day.

The great wealth destruction was accompanied by the fear that everything had changed forever for investors. I will never forget stepping outside onto Fifth Avenue after the close of the market. The sight of women strolling and shopping was so strange. Weren't they aware that the world as we knew it had just ended? On the way to the subway, I passed an attractive woman hawking $50 memberships for the first one hundred members to the newest upscale gym opening in the city. Even though I had not lost money that day, I looked at her and thought to myself, "Who could possibly afford $50 to spend on a gym?" Two months later, I joined the gym for $1,500.

The markets remained wild for some time to follow. As forecast in the film *Terminator*, this was the actual rise of the machines on Wall Street. The Black Monday crash was largely due to computer-generated trading, and I could easily argue that this activity has been at the root of many of the most dramatic declines that followed. Stock market investing is really a pretty straightforward affair. The rational investor looks to buy businesses and participate in their free-cash generation over some future period. If the cash you expect the business to generate over an extended period of time meaningfully exceeds the current price you are being asked to pay for the business, and you deem the risks reasonable, then the stock is a buy. Of course, the inverse is true for selling held positions. That's largely it. When investing activities stray from this singular focus for any prolonged period of time, losses inevitably follow, and when great leverage is added to the mix—as is always the case in periods of plenty—and large, dispassionate machine trading is unleashed, bad things happen. We have had many bouts of such chaos since Black Monday, and I fear that more and larger episodes are sure to follow. Few lessons seem to have been learned.

As a result of liquidating my portfolio, I had my first big victory as an investor, and people noticed. I soon received a great deal of attention from the senior money managers in the firm and eventually chose to join one of the partners in managing his clients' capital.

I didn't know much about Arthur before joining him in business, but when I was being interviewed, he said something I had never heard before. He willingly confessed that he wasn't very good at managing money and would be happy to turn over those efforts to me while he plied his recognized skills in client service and marketing. Humility on Wall Street was not standard fare, and I instantly knew he was different.

Arthur was absolutely magnificent. In a wholly different manner, he was a powerful evolution of those qualities I first observed in my mother. Intellectually, he was really well polished. Whether it was religion, politics, the arts, or ethics, he spoke with great education and great restraint. He was far more interested in the pursuit of knowledge than the easily acquired opinion. He was both intellectually curious and adventurous in search of the values and insights that helped one live a richer, more satisfying life. In so many respects, he helped me explore ideas and ways of living I had never before considered. We had an absolutely glorious time together for the next six years as we tried to create a truly exceptional business.

Equal to his goals for our business was his interest in making me into a person of culture and substance. For this, I cannot be more grateful. Similar to my mother, Arthur held a perspective of a life well lived that was far different than conventional wisdom. His choices were the products of careful deliberation and great personal awareness. Arthur uniquely possessed the quiet confidence needed to plot a course of his own design. His willingness to stand apart was not a statement but a passion to live a life of great substance. He once asked me if I knew the definition of a rich man. After I conceded ignorance, he offered this: "The rich man is the one who is satisfied with his lot." The answer is indisputable, and it was abundantly clear to me that he was a very rich man.

Traces of Arthur's unique character appeared even before one had the chance to meet him. He thought through everything, including his uniquely crafted style of dress. Whether in the halls of business or on a casual stroll in the street, he couldn't be missed. Quick glances at his distinctively patterned three-piece suits, fashionable hats, handkerchiefs, bow ties, ascots, flowers, and all manner of shoes were more than sufficient to gain a clear impression of him. But your impression would be decidedly misplaced. This was just the surface, and Arthur was about anything but the surface. As one of the leaders of an historically important Sephardic synagogue on the Upper West Side of Manhattan, he was a man of deeply held beliefs. Though he was well versed in the traditions, he was thoughtful enough to create practices that married deeply held beliefs with modern interpretations of practice that produced a sense of the orthodox in the contemporary world. And it was his spirituality, curiosity, and creativity that nourished his hunger for the arts.

Arthur and his wife Carol loved and actively attended all manner of artistic performances, including the symphony, the opera, and the ballet. I will never forget the first time they invited my wife Lisa and me to the ballet. As we stood on the elegant balcony during intermission, he was intent on making sure I understood many of the nuances of the performance. To that end, he wanted to show me how they executed the amazing lifts seen during the performance. So here we were, in one of the most elegant places I had ever been, and this man who was a fraction of my size was trying to lift me at the waist and thrust me into the air, despite my vigorous protestations.

Arthur's love for contemporary art exceeded all else. His interest began long before it became fashionable, and he enjoyed the rare privilege of sharing this passion with his equally gifted wife. At one point, Arthur was listed in a book that counted him amongst the two hundred most significant collectors of contemporary art in the world. Not only was this a deeply held love, but Arthur also understood the very important role that conscientious collectors held in financing the lives, careers, and work of the artistic community. He felt the love, as well as the responsibility, of his role in the art world and was an important member of some of the influential institutions in New York.

I remember when Arthur began my education into this fantastic subject matter. He opened with this rather provocative statement: "All the pretty pictures have been painted. The great art is now about ideas, and the creativity and clarity with which those ideas are communicated." For him, art was largely a cerebral affair, and his approach to identifying and researching the rare pieces of great worth was an important inspiration for our investment process.

In keeping with his passion for intellectual integrity, Arthur encouraged me to create a money-management business that ignored convention to find best practices in the art and execution of managing money for long-term client reward. Traditionally, money managers leaned on stock diversification to reduce risk. But after we studied the topic, we concluded that diversification was not a worthy risk-reduction strategy for a stock portfolio. Simply put, when you have a diversified portfolio of stocks, you have a lot of holdings in many different areas of business. As a result, your portfolio of stocks increasingly resembles and performs similarly to the overall market indexes. So if I were to offer the proposition that the market was going to decline 20 percent in the next twelve months, would it be risk-averse to act like the market? No! So we chose a different path.

By the way, this is the principle reason why most active money managers trail the market over time. Their diversified portfolios predetermine that they will perform similarly as the market averages, and then they charge their clients fees, commissions and expenses, depressing their returns relative to the market. To let you in on a big secret, diversification is a more effective risk-reduction tool for the money manager than for his or her clients. The number one goal of any financial advisor is to keep their client assets under management because that is where the fees come from. And most managers are aware that this goal is easier to achieve through good marketing rather than good performance. So when markets decline, it is far more advantageous to claim that everyone is in the same boat rather than try to swim against the tide of poor performance.

We believed that the best way to offer favorable returns for our clients was to reduce trading costs and act independently of the average market performance. After considerable reading and debate, we chose to build a practice based on concentrated investments in a few carefully selected securities. We made great efforts to research our investments extensively and hold them for more than twelve months to gain optimal after-tax rewards. Our strategy was to reduce risks through a detailed understanding of the stocks owned rather than to rely on the general expectation of a rising market. In effect, we decided to accept the risks, rewards, and responsibilities of stock market performance.

That was a real mouthful after having waxed poetic about Arthur. But that was part of his beauty. Arthur could find the same poetry in business as in art, as long as one attached integrity and intellect to the pursuit. Although our finished product did challenge certain aspects of conventional wisdom, it was not our intention to create some grand statement of difference. We simply wished to create a business model that would benefit clients consistent with our studied conclusions. But we soon learned that straying from convention came with costs.

Completely unbeknownst to us, we were the subjects of multiple conversations at executive committee meetings. Even though our performance was consistently outstanding for the first five and a half years, we were labeled "too risky." This label kept us on the outside, away from the firm's considerable resources. In addition, there was one other cost associated with this label: my prospect of achieving partnership was increasingly unlikely. For the longest time we were unaffected by this, because we were happy and completely in the dark. Only much later did a member of the committee choose to share this knowledge with us.

Choosing Arthur was a great decision, but it was also a very telling decision on my part. At the time, I was being interviewed for positions with some of the more powerful partners of the firm, but I chose the different path. Without great forethought, I was attracted to the road less traveled. I always admired the courage and spirit of the underdog, the outsider, the fighter, or the unconventional person. Although I never counted myself among them, the perception of me held by my peers was quite different. My lack of self-awareness and my failure to make the necessary accommodations for my differences would in time prove to undermine many of my ambitions.

Even as I proceeded along a career path that I believed to be full of great promise, I still struggled. Strangely, I could not separate my success from my deep, psychological responsibility to those not privileged enough to join a path of success of their choosing. There seemed to always exist this peculiar cocktail of capitalist dream and social responsibility. They were inseparable, and if some balance beyond my rational understanding were not maintained, I was not at peace. As I continued to make commitments to accommodate both sets of responsibilities, the standards by which I judged myself continued to rise. Not only did I wish to achieve impossibly high levels of performance in the stock market, but I also intended to become a force for social change.

THE OPPORTUNITY
OF A LIFETIME

E verything changed when I received an unsolicited
phone call from a gentleman of considerable influence. He began with the awkward introduction: "I hear
you're a real do-gooder. How would you like to tutor one
of my children?" I did not know who he was, but he got
my name from a friend so I decided to question him
further. I found out that he was part of a well-known
program called the "I Have A Dream" Foundation,
founded by the philanthropist Eugene M. Lang. This
was a wonderful, nationally recognized program that
offered college tuition to entire classes of sixth graders

in disadvantaged schools upon the students' graduation from high school. The program had many great success stories, but this man had identified a simple flaw that he was looking to remedy. Most of these kids didn't have the support systems necessary to stick to a goal requiring years of consistent commitment to achieve. My caller was looking for someone to play the role of tutor/mentor to guide one of his struggling students.

This opportunity was right up my alley. With no plan, no resources, and no time, I countered his offer. "I will tutor all of your kids or none of them." I have no idea why I said this, except that I never seemed to suffer from a lack of confidence, nor could I imagine any reasonable sense of limitations or boundaries. After negotiating a bit, he agreed to let me tutor those students who were struggling, which amounted to about half of his twenty-eight "Dreamers," as they were called.

It was scramble time. I now had fourteen students and no help. What was my next move? I needed more tutors and a place to make it happen. I turned to my firm and begged them to let me bring the students to our workplace twice a week to be tutored by willing employees. Begrudgingly, they agreed. My next job was to find willing employees and train them. This took some arm-twisting and a considerable commitment of time, but steadily, enthusiasm and participation grew. My firm proved to be a wonderful incubator for ideas, practices, and disciplines that I would use for years to come.

After successfully bringing my firm onboard, I immediately began to prepare for the expansion of the program. With the wonderful assistance of my wife, we attracted about ten different businesses of great stature to participate. Among them were some of the most powerful firms in the legal community and on Wall Street. Leaning on my prior experiences, I put together training manuals for the tutors and created rules and disciplines for all involved to ensure safe and enjoyable learning environments. After extraordinary success with the first group of students, two more "I Have A Dream" classes asked for my assistance. Later, the Manhattan Institute, a conservative think tank interested in educational issues and solutions, solicited me to do work directly with some of the more progressive at-risk schools in Harlem.

The program was complex to administer, but one simple decision made for all the successes that followed.. Rather than have the tutors go to the students' schools, we had the students come to the tutors' places of employment. Recruitment was easier, and tutors were more reliable and generous with their time. The tutors looked forward to their sessions, and many employees who were not initially aligned with the program looked to participate. We paired two adults with each child to vary the experiences and ensure that a tutor was always available. As a consequence, we eventually involved close to one thousand adults through the course of the program. It was obvious to me that people wanted to give, and it was our responsibility to make it easy for them. We did, they were great, and the kids reaped the benefits.

For the students, this structure was life changing. Most of these kids had never been in an office building. It was unlikely that they knew someone who dressed in a suit for work, and they had few if any relationships with adults of different races and backgrounds. Crossing these boundaries and being exposed to new experiences catalyzed incredible learning experiences that changed their dreams and prospects. We asked them to be responsible and did not tolerate excessive tardiness or absenteeism. There were simply too many deserving children waiting to join. We expected the students to be prepared, behave respectfully, dress appropriately, and participate enthusiastically. Imaginations were challenged. Bias was challenged. And horizons and aspirations were changed.

This journey lasted much of the next ten years and was possibly the greatest experience of my life. In a tribute to its roots, I named it the "American Dream Project." I was doing something that eventually touched four hundred students but had the potential to help infinitely more as the partnerships between each participating business and the associated educational institutions became self-sustaining and self-administering. Schools, workplaces, and lives were changed forever.

Placing a motivated child in a relationship with a resource-rich, generous adult is the simplest formula for long-term change. When speaking of resources, I am referring to the term in the broadest context imaginable. Giving money is great, but giving love, attention, and guidance is of incalculable worth. And, just as we had hoped, the tutors and their businesses gained meaningful collateral advantage. In a world where loyalty is constantly eroding, enriching the business environment with meaningful charitable activity can be a vital source of competitive difference. Pride in the workplace can be an important differentiator for employee retention, employee recruitment, productivity improvements, and customer engagement.

A powerful example I can share from my own experience involved our large and profitable pension-management business. On one nondescript afternoon, the senior partner responsible for managing our pension business stopped me to talk. I was cautious, because this guy was particularly unwelcoming and had never previously bothered even to look in my direction. Unexpectedly, he offered his thanks. Apparently, several large pension-fund accounts that were under review by clients decided to stay with our firm after reading an article about the American Dream Project that was featured in *The New York Times*. Knowing the business as I did, performance advantages between one fund and another are often razor-thin, and retaining business is very difficult. As this example demonstrated, our firm retained a large sum of business because clients wished to be associated with a firm that had gained a reputation for charitable behavior and actions. These client decisions were worth millions of dollars of fees to our firm.

This was just one example. For all the companies involved in our project, the opportunity to publicize their involvement was a real plus. And, from my perspective, that was exactly as it should be. If I could get people to act selfishly for the greater good, I had a formula for success that could spread. Principals received recognition for their schools, kids graduated and went to college, and businesses created goodwill and made more money. All I had to do was get in the middle of it all and coax, cajole, and challenge. Most importantly, there were no monetary costs to anyone. I took all the friction out of the system so that the students and volunteers were free to learn and grow.

There were however two non-monetary costs that someone had to be willing to assume to make this work: time and personal risk. In general, this program took up half my workdays, and I was fortunate to have a boss who was okay with that. In addition, there was the issue of personal liability. My wife worked at a law firm and they generously created a contract for the program which all the students and guardians were required to sign. But as we all know, with four hundred students moving around the subways to different places of business at different times, there was always a risk of something happening and our being sued. I took extraordinary pains to orchestrate times, conditions, and rules of engagement to keep everyone safe. Thankfully, nothing bad ever happened.

I would like to make one further editorial comment about my charitable experiences to date. I believe that the simple ideas of proximity and resource transfer are the key concepts to constructing durable social change. Proximity is the driving force of connection. Vital human connection fails to take root without the ability to engage our senses. When we learn of things remotely, the emotions stirred are fleeting, but when we can feel, touch, communicate, and empathize directly, connection acquires new meaning, and personal differences prove to be far less formidable boundaries. Most importantly, when connection is facilitated, the fertile ground of common cause and the feelings of shared interests create the basis for dialogue and understanding. People are no longer foreign but familiar. This is when involvement shifts from sympathy to action. Sharing money is fine, but sharing the rich spectrum of gifts and talents—including family, friendship, love, and understanding—can enrich everyone involved beyond our imaginations. All that is required is energy, enthusiasm, and the ability to truly advocate on behalf of all the involved constituencies.

And this is the key point: everyone's interests must be given equal attention if we are ever to achieve genuine and sustainable engagement. I put just as much effort into romancing the tutors and businesses as I did the students and schools. If we create programs that drive meaningful personal face-to-face engagement between businesses, students and teachers, Blacks, Whites, Asians, Latinos, and so on, consistently, for long periods of time, we would have better businesses, better students, better workers, and ultimately, better citizens.

In my opinion, that is how you construct lasting social change. We need proximity, not policy, to overcome the intractable barriers we have constructed. New York City was the most fascinating laboratory for my little experiment. On one side of 96th Street on the East Side of Manhattan there resides some of our poorest citizens and on the other, some of our wealthiest. Divided by a mere twenty feet of concrete, each side heeds this boundary as if it were twenty miles. It is this metaphorical distance that allows fear to overwhelm understanding and enables rhetoric to build barriers that make it easy to demonize and grow apart. A rich appreciation for all that underlies the meaning of true proximity is the only solution that will fundamentally catalyze understanding, dialogue, and trust, leading to durable social change.

BACK TO BUSINESS

As the American Dream Project gained momentum, so did our money-management business. My relationship with Arthur was a joy. The environment he created was incredible, and our business thrived. This was no small accomplishment because he and I were operating somewhat on the periphery of the firm. Our investment strategy was different than the rest of the firm and we were excluded from the firm's professional marketing efforts. In addition, we were not allowed to use any of the research or investment banking services offered to the firm by the large Wall Street brokerage houses. Relative to many of our peers, both inside and outside the firm, we were operating at a significant disadvantage. So, as our client list grew and our stock market performance excelled, we shared an extraordinary sense of pride and satisfaction.

After a period of sustained success, I received an unexpected call from the managing partner of our firm. When I arrived at his office, I was surprised to see the head of our institutional investment business there to join the conversation. Without preamble, they launched into a discussion of our stock market accomplishments and, with little transition, they asked if I would be willing to manage a pension fund for the firm. This was essentially our invitation into the firm's institutional business, including the valuable research and trading privileges we had previously been denied.

I was flattered but, at the same time, cautious. I guess the rushed nature of the meeting and the noticeable absence of Arthur put me back on my heels. Before I could ask my first question, they offered one caveat: although impressed with our performance, they wanted to know if I would be willing to manage the pension fund in a style more consistent with the other managers in the firm. My immediate response was to pose the following logical observation: "If I were to alter our strategy, I could not be sure that our performance would remain exceptional." That was okay with them, but for some reason, my instincts suggested that it should not be fine with me. After a very brief and somewhat antiseptic conversation, I politely declined.

Despite the strange construction of the meeting, after a brief moment of hesitation, most would have rebounded quickly and enjoyed feelings of validation and accomplishment. I, on the other hand, distinctly recall my early reaction as being one of offense. Rather than focusing on the praise, rather than considering the bigger opportunity, my mind immediately closed ranks as I fixated on their choice to not use our strategy. My self-image was so tightly identified with all the products of my labor that any rejection was total rejection. Rather than negotiate, explore their thinking more deeply, ask for more time, or request that Arthur join us, I simply declined. I would rather show strength and attach myself to our independence than compromise and concede. I had completely bought into our struggle as outsiders and our accomplishments as being worthy of some David-and-Goliath moment.

There is nothing wrong with being proud of success, but my reaction was different. Rather than accept the privileges offered as a reward for our performance, I pivoted to protect our business from some form of camouflaged attack. What should have been understood as an opportunity for our business was suddenly interpreted as a threat to all we had achieved. Trust was replaced by caution and fear, and dialogue was replaced by reaction.

In many respects, I was overly attached to the identity of being associated with a worthy struggle and was ill prepared to see the struggle end. I had formed a self-image that I believed to be characterized by strength and independence, but when exposed to the harsh light of reality, it revealed a rigid bearing that would ultimately make expectations unrealizable and failure intolerable.

There was another side to this story that only first became visible when I began writing this book. I was raised with a healthy skepticism of privilege, a disdain for elitism, and a general distrust of the wealthy. I recall walking through one of my mother's first big architectural jobs. The client was very wealthy, the setting was beautiful, and my mother had a very free hand to be creative. She was proud of the work and was anxious to share and discuss. But as soon as the tour was over, her temperament changed. She turned to my sister and me and, said, "Remember, no one in this family is happy."

She wanted us to understand that money had nothing to do with happiness. On its own, it's a valid and worthy point. But there is a difference between correcting a misperception and constructing a code. Over time, her messages seemed to connect wealth, privilege, and power with unhappiness, as well as a host of other equally unattractive qualities. On this point, she was relentless. If you happened to have dinner at a well-known restaurant, traveled in deluxe accommodations, or made a luxury purchase, it was best to temper your description of the purchase or experience. Because if your guard eased and an honest remark slipped recalling your enjoyment of the particular indulgence, the cutting response from my mother was delivered with ninja-like speed and accuracy. It was critically important to Mom that both my sister and I always think and act within a framework that considered those less fortunate first.

I had always thought that I had navigated this somewhat peculiar upbringing with relative ease. I listened, participated, and moved on, never feeling particularly attached or affected. But I now know that was not the case. As we all went forward, our unconventional brand of family values proved easier for the others in my family to accommodate. Mom worked in a world where her peculiarity was an asset that was admired. For Dad, it was perfect. He didn't talk much, and his clients' mouths were fully occupied when in his presence. And my sister became a therapist whose work involved caring for the children of the wealthy. So she was helping others as well as validating all of my mother's most deeply held biases concerning the problems of families with wealth.

My experience was very different. My career was directly in the line of sight of all the negative messaging with which I had been raised. My business was all about money and money was how people measured success and acquired power. I was in the money business and my psyche had been encoded with an abundance of bias and distrust for the people and institutions that I now depended upon for my success. And in my line of work, difference was given a very short leash. I was unaware of the conflict created by these biases and was unprepared to make any thoughtful compensation.

When I walked into that meeting with the managing partner you can bet my guard was up. And although this may be a reasonable posture when taking an unexpected business meeting with a powerful person, in my case the skepticism came from a far deeper source. I was trained to withhold my trust in such a circumstance amongst such people. And when I detected the smallest anomaly, I was programmed to recoil. As a result, when the opportunity I had long been chasing finally surfaced, I was ill equipped to accept, accommodate and capitalize. The deck was stacked against me before I even took my seat at the table.

REFLECTION

Although the arc of my career would remain intact for years to come, I believe this meeting with the managing partner was the moment when my trajectory of growth changed. The business we created was an important personal milestone. The struggle to get from Westbury to a place of great stature was complete, and our record of performance was the proof statement needed to validate my accomplishment. We had designed a product from the ground up; we were unafraid to be unconventional and we succeeded. But when they opened the door to acknowledge our success, I could not walk through it.

I had found a business partner I loved and respected, but that was not enough. We had gotten some measure of validation from peers, but that was not enough. We were offered entry into the mainstream, but the lure of the unconventional was more appealing. We were being offered shelter from some of the risks of working in the most volatile business by joining the firm's institutional efforts, but I preferred to face the elements head-on, without a safety net.

Reaching a place where one could gain shelter from the market was the aspiration of all the successful operators in the business. Although I had not yet gained such a position, gaining the support, services, and backing of the larger institution was certainly an important step in the right direction. And while I wanted that, I wanted it on my terms. I was distrustful of convention and was wed to a self-image that wanted to be tested under the harsh lights of objective numbers. And I operated under the misguided belief that I was perfectly fine on my own.

On a deeper level, this was my response to the privileged. This was my message to kids driving Cadillac cars to school. Let's measure up and see who deserves what. Deep in my soul I believed that any help would diminish what I had accomplished and dilute the message I wished to send. The anger I held inside was far greater than I understood. And I used an inflated sense of self-confidence as both a shield and a weapon.

Unfortunately, that strategy only served to distance me from allies of great worth and left my circumstances untenable and fragile. Failure was inevitable and the fall was going to be hard.

At the very end of my tenure of managing money at this institution, my performance stumbled for two months, damaging our performance. I was crushed. I was so invested in maintaining a pristine record of performance that when our investments began to falter and replacements were not easily found, rather than accept modest losses and lagging performance, I held on and hoped for the best. I felt trapped by my expectations of unfaltering exceptional performance when, in fact, I was not trapped at all. I had produced over five consecutive years of great numbers. I should have easily been willing to accept one mediocre year when ideas were not abundant. But I could not.

Instead, I spied failure when no signs of failure could be reasonably found. And I traded action for reaction when action was called for. I was a prisoner of my own design and I believed that any failure was total failure. And when I stumbled I could not forgive myself. I was sad that I had let my partner and our clients down. And I was embarrassed by my failure. Working among my peers was no longer an option for me, so I chose to leave the firm. I was filled with regret about my experience, and for many years, I was unable to recall any memories of success or happiness. In retrospect, the cost I paid to leave the firm was manageable. However, the cost I paid to leave Arthur was astronomical.

Arthur is one of the finest human beings I have ever met, and leaving him behind for all the business experiences yet to come was not nearly adequate compensation. He was a person I truly trusted and respected, and he was capable of helping me grow and evolve into the balanced person I needed to become. He was the teacher of lessons I desperately required, but I was not yet the student who was capable of learning all that he had to offer. Although he remained a part of my life for the next few years, I didn't maintain the required energy to keep the relationship fertile. My life is infinitely richer for having learned from him and infinitely sadder for not keeping him in it.

I recall a most revealing story from my early days with him. I was sitting in his office when a senior partner of the firm interrupted us to show Arthur his latest acquisition of art. As he scrambled around his desk to share the photographs of the piece, Arthur was very liberal with his praise for the acquisition. After the senior partner left the office, most satisfied with the response, I noticed that Arthur's demeanor had changed as he quietly shook his head. At this time, as wealth was growing rapidly for all of Wall Street, the acquisition of art was an important marker of status. So when I asked Arthur about his obvious change of mood, he remarked, "He's doing what he's supposed to do, not what he wants to do." There it is. There was no authenticity, no love, no passion—simply a desire to be validated by his peers.

Unfortunately, as I reflect back on my last days, I see signs of the same lack of authenticity and direction. As advancement in the firm became more tenuous, I was quick to dispatch all we had achieved. The true worth of our relationship and our accomplishments faded, and validation from others was now assigned a greater priority. With my bearings lost, I scrambled to find safe shores. Time would prove that all that was gained was little compared to all that was lost.

MATTERS OF TRUST

If I pause our discussion and return to the first few pages of this book, the answers to the questions posed come into better focus. For the vast majority of my life I was completely unaware of a personal style that my friend so cleverly described as "Greg against the world." I had developed a disposition that valued strength not vulnerability, independence not cooperation, confidence not compromise, and obligations to others not obligation to self. And although many of these traits are admirable, they also portray a person that is often alone, inflexible, and in general has a difficult time with trust.

And when you combine this personal style or code with the distrust of wealth, privilege and power learned as a youth, it offers powerful context underlying my gut reaction to turn down the managing partner's proposal rather than accept his warm welcome. To join the pension management business of my firm required that I trust the intentions and commitments of those who offered me the position. It required that I trust that their proposal was offered with my interests in mind. And it required that I be willing to cede some elements of control over my investment strategies, performance and career to executives and an institution that I had not yet learned to trust. It was all matters of trust that led me to walk away from an opportunity that I was indirectly chasing my entire adult life.

My unwillingness to trust regulated the risks I was willing to take and the choices I was free to make. Trust changed the direction of my life and I was completely unaware of the awesome power and influence invested in this quality of our character.

A great friend and valued advisor once told me that the truly gifted person is capable of learning great lessons from small mistakes rather than having to suffer great mistakes before one can learn the great lessons. Unfortunately, I was not amongst the truly gifted.

TRANSITIONS

Despite appearances, the work experiences that followed were generally struggles. My performance and work ethic were consistently praised and my efforts were rewarded with partnerships and, in some cases, substantial compensation. But for some reason, that was never enough. It was always too easy for me to spy the disingenuous, to expose the false pretense, and to uncover the priority accorded to image over substance. There was a constant itch just beneath the surface of my skin arguing that this very serious financial game was not done with the honesty of purpose that it deserved.

I think that, in my heart, I always was looking to find a good replacement for Arthur, and that just wasn't going to happen. My position with my first investment house had lasted almost thirteen years and, in large part, was a place that offered so many of the qualities I deeply desired. But as I tried to fill the gaps in my places of employment that followed, I ended up experiencing more loss than gain. Although I honestly thought that I found positions that would offer new challenges and enhance my spectrum of skills and experiences, the reality was often very different. Oftentimes, the reputation and mission statements of the institutions were far from revealing of the true intellectual and business experience offered. In retrospect, what I learned was that the quality of the professional experience was largely a function of the energy, motivations, and trust shared with those with whom you share responsibility and to whom you report. In this regard, nothing came close to my relationship with Arthur.

My search for a place of growth and opportunity came to an abrupt conclusion with my last formal post. I was introduced to this new opportunity through excellent channels. His references were good and his track record was worthy. The fundamental underpinnings of a good business relationship were all in place. However, for the first time, something was different. Prior to this, every venture I had entered filled me with the excitement of dynamic prospects. Optimism, enthusiasm, and energy were commodities in abundant supply. But this time, my body was sending a distinctly different vibe. Something was wrong, but I couldn't put my finger on it. Because I wanted to keep working, with no other alternatives in sight, I ignored my instincts and marshaled on, hoping for the best. Little did I know the magnitude of the costs I would suffer because of my failure to listen to the subtle voices speaking to me from within.

We did the traditional dance for a few months before deciding to engage all the resources needed to get our business off the ground. Having done this courtship process before, I knew its basic flaw. In the investment business, it is very hard to forecast how people will perform or conduct themselves before you start investing real dollars. Risk is not a theoretical exercise, thus any preliminary academic exercise to judge strategy and execution is largely nonsense because investing without risk is fundamentally absurd. So when my new partner insisted that we sign a three-year operating agreement prior to opening the business as a show of commitment, my biology was broadcasting clear signs of alarm. But I stayed committed to what I wished for, rather than aware of what I was feeling.

It was amazing how fast I knew I had made a big mistake soon after we began investing. I was not concerned that our investing styles and strategies were very different; that was often a point of strength in this business. The problem was squarely rooted in our response to the differences. I welcomed the differences and wanted to trust that two seasoned professionals could conduct their affairs independently with commonality of purpose and mutual advantage. But my partner's response was entirely different. His immediate response to all differences was to try to assert control. It was clear from the beginning that he was incapable of trusting difference, and he tried to enforce practices that gave him considerable influence over all of our investment activities.

Our engagement with a business therapist was a most telling example of what I was forced to endure. After several months of conflict, my partner insisted that we see a therapist he had used in the past who specialized in counseling partners experiencing difficult working relationships. I was reticent but, as usual, I relented. After several sessions filled with conflict, the therapist asked us each to bring to the next session a written statement describing our ideas of practices and principles of a healthy working arrangement. When I whipped out my three-page document, hoping to find a way forward, my partner stated that he had not brought anything to the session. Later, he confessed that he had never really wished nor intended to compromise. The only conclusion I could reach was that this entire exercise was organized to steer me to his original wishes. Using therapy as a tool to manipulate seemed like a devious bastardization of its intended purpose. That was our last session.

THE WATERSHED
MOMENT

As with most important business engagements, there were highs and lows. Commonly, it is not until the final days that simply coming to work is hard to endure. But in this last business experience, many of those feelings were front and center from the beginning. The stress was enormous. I distinctly recall the dread I felt each day as I opened the front door, hoping he was not there. When that wasn't the case, I felt trapped and limited. We had signed a contract that obliged us to work together for three years, and that prospect was frightening. Intellectually, psychologically, and emotionally, I was running on empty. Then I met Kevin.

Soon after we launched our business, we moved into new office space in Manhattan. I remember moving day. It was a Monday, and my partner knew that I had passed my second-degree black belt test the day before, so he jokingly said to the office manager who helped us move in, "You better do what Greg says. He's a second-degree black belt."

Instead of being impressed, the office manager, Kevin, responded, "Really? I'm an eighth-degree black belt. You want to work out some time so I can see what you got?" I immediately said yes, and we began working out that first week.

Kevin is an amazing guy. He had traveled around the country fighting in sponsored mixed martial arts tournaments before the sport gained its current popularity. Kevin had amassed a record of seventy-nine wins and zero losses in his fights and he told me that he had wanted to get to one hundred wins, until diabetes forced him to retire. Instead, he continued his personal development while training fighters. In fact, some of his fighters could be seen on television, competing in the big-sports productions. Kevin was very serious and trained with many of the greats in New York, including Tiger Schulman and the Gracie brothers. So it was incredibly flattering to hear how impressed he was with my skills.

We began training religiously, three to four days a week. Training with Kevin was the real deal. We often began by running seventy-five timed flights of stairs, followed by jumping rope, fighting specific exercises, bag work, and sparring. Each session was one- to-two hours in length; there were no breaks, and there was very limited rest. The learning experience was very complex, requiring precision footwork, carefully choreographed body motions, and exacting angles for delivering kicks and punches.

Not only was it physically taxing, but it was mentally challenging as well. I could not possibly have had more fun, and I anxiously awaited all his criticism and approval. This was by far the brightest part of my day and provided a necessary release valve from the constant tension and anger of the workday. Physically and emotionally, my daily schedule was pretty gruesome: a one-and-a-half-hour commute to work, a full day of emotional stress working with my partner, extreme physical stress while working with Kevin, and then the commute home. I'm sure I was not properly honoring the wear and tear processed over the previous fifty-two years of my life, especially when one considers the extra corrosion that accompanies a stressful career on Wall Street.

After following this routine for about a year, my family and I went on a ski vacation. A little background is required. I had the good fortune of skiing since I was five years old, a great byproduct of my father being stationed in Bangor, Maine, for his tour in the military. Mom and Dad had learned to ski and were addicted.

We didn't have much extra money to spend growing up, but they always found the funds for the annual family ski trip to Vermont.

This was real, no-frills stuff, including nine hours of fighting with my sister in the back seat of the car, AM radio only, modest accommodations, and mountains that were generally more ice than snow. But this was the best thing that happened to us every year. One notable feature was the bonding time I had with Dad. As I've already described, Dad was not a big talker and in the early days he was sometimes a bit unapproachable as he stressed about money. But when we were skiing, all that went away. Skiing was our great common ground. All we did was talk skiing all day, every day. It was the place where we genuinely came together, and the memories of those trips have not faded one bit.

Fortunately, I was able to carry on that tradition with my family, and it was the same endless source of fun. On this particular trip, the kids were skiing at their best and begged me to lead them down a double-black-diamond, heavy-powder tree run for the last ski adventure of the trip. If you don't know skiing lingo, all that gibberish can be translated to mean a really tough ski run. And everyone who has ever skied knows the bad luck associated with the last run of the vacation. Despite my better judgment, we gave it a shot.

A funny thing can happen on a late-afternoon powder run. In the bright Colorado sun, even on the coldest days, the top layer of snow tends to melt, and as the sun fades, a thin layer of crust forms on top. This makes the snow very tough to manipulate, making safety a real concern. The top half of the run was the most difficult, and everyone managed very nicely. So, as things were getting easier, I let my guard down, allowing myself to relax and pick up pace.

Now is a good time for your second snow lesson. If you look at the base of a tree in heavy snow, you will often find a ring of loose and light snow right around its trunk. This is referred to as the "well" of the tree. Because of this variable snow pattern, if you get too close, your ski can feel like it is getting drawn in toward the tree trunk. As I was picking up speed, I hit a modest jump and landed too close to a pine tree. Instantaneously, my ski veered hard to the right, lining my head up with the center of the tree. Bang!

I can still see it all very clearly. Fortunately, I was sufficiently athletic to fold my left knee in front of me to soften the blow. The next thing I remember, I was on my back, and everything was spinning, lights were flashing, and the pain was through the roof. But the worst part was that when I regained my vision, I saw my kids crying. There was blood, and I thought my leg was broken, but I had to steady the kids. I rallied quickly and told them I was okay. Fortunately, my brother-in-law had joined us and was strong enough to pick me up out of the heavy snow and get me back on my feet. Knowing how hard it would be to get the rescue people up to this remote spot, I told everyone I could ski down. A bit bloody and only able to put weight on one leg, I made it down to find my wife waiting to take me to the medical center.

A brief aside before we continue: at the time of the accident, I had been skiing for forty-eight years and was a very capable skier. Although there had been many injuries and close calls, none remotely compared to this. So here's the interesting thing. During all of those forty-eight years, despite the constant urging of my entire family, this was the first time I had ever worn a helmet. A little spooky, don't you think? I think that helmet may have been the difference between life and death. Later, I told this story to a friend and personal advisor who always seems to see things a bit differently. His first reaction was to point out that I might have hit the tree *because* I was wearing the helmet. A little spooky, don't you think?

When I got to the medical center, I was scared. I had always been able to count on the good health of my body and was really fearful of what I might learn. I knew that I had blacked out for a few moments, so a concussion was a distinct possibility. I also understood the possibility that my leg was injured, but beyond that, I was unaware of what else might be wrong. The only thing I knew for sure was that I wanted out of there.

It turned out that my leg was not broken. Using the shinbone as a shield had been a good move. But the wide gash on my shin from ankle to knee provided ample evidence of the violence of the accident. After my leg was patched up, I answered every question with a lie manufactured to get out of there, and following a relatively short inspection I got my wish. I had headaches, my knee was clearly damaged, and my body was very shaky, but we were leaving the next day and I wanted to go home.

When I got home, we went right to our naturopath who, upon examination, insisted I see a cardiologist immediately. This experience was very unsettling. I knew little about serious health issues, and when I arrived at the cardiologist's office, the first thing I noticed was that I was the only person under the age of one hundred. What was I doing here? He put me on the treadmill, and shortly thereafter, he shouted at the nurse to stop the machine. When I told him I was fine, he countered that I was not fine. Within the first minute, my heart rate was already clocking well north of two hundred beats per minute. He then mentioned something about A-Fib and was talking about shocking my heart and giving me drugs. It was all far too much for me to handle. I remember refusing all of his advice and walking out of the office, until I heard the nurse's voice as she chased me down the hall: "You better take this seriously, or you could die!" All of a sudden, everything got real.

Just to define our terms, A-Fib is an irregular and often rapid, heartbeat that increases the risk of stroke, heart failure and other heart related complications. About 15-20% of people who have strokes have this condition. Common feelings are a pounding in the chest, nausea, dizziness, fatigue and shortness of breath. There are different types of A-Fib and its cause remains unclear. Currently, there are treatments that can address certain symptoms, but there are no treatments that offer a "cure."

I returned to work, with all the associated tension, and resumed my training with Kevin, minus the kicks, because my leg was not working well at all. Increasingly, my naturopath was counseling caution and strongly advised that I discontinue training. I really had no choice because even modest exercise made my pulse race and I had no energy to bring to my sessions with Kevin. The limitations were very frustrating.

There was, however, one bright spot. I was able to convince my partner that our relationship was literally killing me, and he kindly released me from our three-year commitment. I was free, but free to do what? I did not know. I knew that I had come to a watershed moment, and my mind was racing as fast as my heart.

PART 2

A BRIEF LOOK BACK

Several years prior to my skiing accident, a set of un-expected circumstances led our family to explore alternative health practices. And with the understanding of the health challenges that I was soon to face, I feel so fortunate that we chose this new direction.

One afternoon, my wife received a call from the principal's office at our son's school. Apparently, Ben had been disruptive in class and required some intervention. Lisa and I were shocked. We had both steered clear of the principal's office in our school years, and the tones of our voices must have betrayed our sense of alarm, prompting the principal to reply, "Oh, you didn't know? He's one of our frequent fliers." A frequent flier!

More detailed conversations revealed that Ben had been having some real behavior problems in elementary school.

We immediately began the search for any and all therapies that could help with our newest challenge. Eventually we secured an appointment with a highly regarded child psychiatrist. Our first visit went smoothly, ending with the doctor pronouncing, "Nothing is wrong. He seems to be a normal, happy kid." But at the next visit, Ben was not at his best, and the doctor was quick to forcefully argue for Ritalin. At the time, Lisa and I had nothing against conventional medicine or the use of conventional drugs. But we had just completed two visits resulting in two opposing diagnoses, followed by what we deemed to be a kneejerk recommendation of medication. Sensing our hesitation, the psychiatrist recommended three books on the subjects of ADD and pronounced confidently that we would see our son on each and every page. Lisa read all three books and didn't recognize Ben once. We never went back.

We continued our research and continued to seek help, but we found ourselves no closer to an answer or to anyone we could trust. It was then that a colleague of mine recommended that we see a naturopathic doctor. We had never heard of the term "naturopathic doctor," and were only vaguely familiar with the idea of alternative medicine.

On our first visit the doctor dove right in. She began by taking a number of different biological samples and ordering an enormous number of tests. In addition, she conducted several tests that were completely new to us, such as muscle testing, energy testing, and skin testing, amongst others. It was the most comprehensive examination either of us had ever experienced. Anxious for her recommendations, we called the doctor. Her preference was to wait for all the results, but we were desperate, so with some preliminary blood work in hand, she offered that Ben had low levels of carbon dioxide in his blood. She thought that if we gave him some carbonated apple juice, it should help. What? Whoever heard of such a thing? Was this lady nuts? Should we trust her? We soon learned that this doctor was not big on bedside manner: "Either do it or don't. It's your decision." Then she hung up.

We gave Ben the juice three times a day, and after a week, we received calls from both his teacher and the principal asking about the drugs we were giving him. According to both, he was a completely different kid. To tell you the truth, we thought this idea about carbon dioxide was complete nonsense, but it cost us nothing to give it a try while we waited for the remaining test results.

When all the diagnostic information became available, our naturopath determined that Ben was suffering from a number of different allergies and other sensitivities. In her judgment, his disruptive behavior was likely in response to his frequent allergic reactions that made him feel like he was uncomfortable in his own skin. He probably needed to move around in class to help relieve his feelings of constant irritation. After completing her treatments, his behavior problems largely disappeared.

One very important observation is worthy of mention: Ben was unaware that either of us was concerned. We were very careful to hide our feelings and we presented all of these visits as routine medical visits for a child his age. And there certainly was nothing revealing about asking a ten year old to drink sparkling apple juice three times a day. In fact, he and all his friends loved the stuff. His remarkable response to treatment was, in our opinion, entirely authentic, and this was evidence we could not ignore.

This entire episode taught Lisa and me an incredibly important lesson that changed our perspective of healthcare. The psychiatrist was anxious to quickly suppress the symptoms of Ben's behavior problems, rather than make a sincere effort to understand the underlying causes. This was the easy way to dispense with the problem. Fix the optics and everyone should be satisfied. Well, we were far from satisfied. And the psychiatrist's apparent disregard for the long-term unintended consequences of drug therapy was very disturbing. In stark contrast, our naturopath investigated the problem without bias and followed the data to explore different treatment options. She was much more interested in cause rather than effects and in the end created a long-term plan that helped fortify Ben's overall health.

Many years later Ben began a career as a successful professional actor. When he learned of this story he thanked us both for looking beyond the easy solution. You see, Ben believes his success as an actor is intimately related to his ability to connect with all of his emotions. And he believes the drugs would have left him disconnected from many of the emotions that he has counted on to become a successful actor.

In time, we ported our entire family to this new brand of medicine, and we could not have been more satisfied. This change took a bit of courage. There are many forces invested with considerable authority, strongly warning against any move away from the mainstream. But the more we learned, the more we knew we would never go back. At the core of many of these non-traditional approaches to healthcare is the belief that all aspects of a person's health must be addressed to produce durable, therapeutic change. The psychological, emotional, and spiritual elements of health are accorded the same attention as the physical elements of good health.

Our children, who began as reluctant participants, now ask for appointments with their various alternative practitioners when they sense the need. For the past decade, our family has experienced little sickness and has required the use of very few drugs. Interestingly, many of the nutritional choices we made years earlier have recently become recommendations of the traditional healthcare community.

From our perspective, Western medicine was obsessed with uncovering disease to apply the next drug, versus the East, which was focused on empowering good health to enable the body to fight the next disease. Consider that, in the early days of Chinese medicine, it was customary to pay your doctor a nominal sum each day you were in good health, and care was free when you were ill. Think of the incentives and behaviors such a system would motivate. Yes, I know that in principle one could ascribe similar motivations to Western health insurance, but all of us who participate in this system know that it does not remotely serve to promote good health in its practical application. In the Chinese model, the incentive was good health. In the current Western model, the incentive is profit.

Around this same time, as a result of a completely unrelated set of circumstances, my wife decided that I needed a hobby. When Father's Day arrived, she presented me with a gift certificate for twelve karate lessons. I am not sure how she came up with this idea, but she was right. This subtle addition to my life would end up being seismic in scope.

On my first day of karate class, I met Al. He was a fourth-degree black belt and had been involved in many different forms of martial arts for over thirty years. He was warm and inviting, and he possessed a natural sense of curiosity and humor. In the dojo, where rank can create the basis for real barriers, Al would have none of it. He took the time to get to know me while helping me get acclimated. We hit it off immediately. He loved the stock market, where I had trained for over twenty years, and for decades, both he and his wife had lived and studied all forms of alternative healthcare and spirituality—the exact thing I was seeking.

Coincidentally, I had been reading theological texts, with the help and guidance of some thoughtful rabbis, for the past ten years. Just before meeting Al, I had come to a bit of a crossroad. After a year of regular study with one particular orthodox rabbi, I shared my conundrum about worship: "If I don't have a view of God, I find it difficult to find meaning in a prayer book overwhelmingly devoted to honoring God." He agreed, without offering any course of remedy. As a result, my studies slowed, and I looked for a new direction. Fortunately, the universe responded by introducing me to Al.

I had not previously considered nontraditional spiritual reading and had just begun to scratch the surface of my non-traditional healthcare study because of our recent experience with our son. And now, with my readings at an impasse, I was eager to get started with my new friend and advisor. Al supplied the reading list and we were in constant dialogue, with karate sessions three times a week in addition to frequent meetings outside the dojo. Our conversations on health, nutrition, and belief were infinitely interesting, and my appetite was voracious. His counsel would prove invaluable.

WITHER OR CHANGE

In my early years on Wall Street, I had the good fortune of befriending a famous strategist. His unenviable job was to publish predictions regarding the direction of the stock market. Unlike many others, he had the intellect to handle the assignment and had generally met with great success. I happened to be attending a large investor conference during a particularly challenging time in the market, and my friend was struggling. As I walked through the crowd, I saw him in the distance and made my way over. I remember greeting him with the conventional "How are you doing?" to which he replied, "I think if I jump out of that window, I'm pretty sure I would go up." I don't recall ever hearing a remark so funny and yet so insightful. Unfortunately, now I, too, was experiencing similar feelings of vertigo and felt completely unsure of each and every step I took.

When there is no clear direction from which to launch or nothing firm to grasp, you rely on your instincts to shake the feeling of paralysis. My first instinct had always been to simply work hard, but that begs the question: work at what? I knew I was broken, but I didn't understand what needed fixing. My career seemed to be over long before I wished it to be. I could no longer exercise or train as I faced the realities of my health issues. I spent months alone, depressed and embarrassed by my circumstance, endlessly processing my mistakes and misfortune. My self-confidence was gone, I felt defeated and I was completely lacking in energy and motivation.

The calls to pull yourself up by your bootstraps or appreciate all that you have fall somewhat on deaf ears when your mind and emotions are racing in search of safe harbor. In this place of insecurity and doubt, putting yourself out there in the world—where trust and good faith are the most important currencies of exchange—was very unsettling.

I spent a long time punishing myself. I was to blame and there needed to be consequences I could feel. I did 1000 pushups a day just to challenge my heart to respond. It did. It got worse. I spent all my time alone in my home office, lights off, unwilling to take any phone calls. Lisa would come up and try to help but I just wasn't ready to listen. And when I joined the family for dinner, everyone knew and everyone kept quiet. There was no end game, no strategy to come out of this funk. I just knew I deserved this and that's the way it would be until something changed.

And then Al called. I had been out of touch and he wanted to check in. He was the one person I couldn't turn away. When he heard what was going on, he insisted I come over immediately. As soon as I arrived, I finally felt safe and broke down. I was fortunate to have known Al for a long time. And I was fortunate that we had spent the vast majority of our time together discussing things of great personal meaning and consequence. So when I arrived at his door, he had a wealth of background at his disposal and I had an abundance of trust.

Al quickly understood what I was doing and he was quick to counsel that I was doing everything wrong. His worldview was predicated on learning, growth and change. My strategy of isolation was all about shutting down and tuning out. His disciplines were designed to tune your body and mind to become highly aware. By punishing myself, I was engaged in practices that shuttered the prospect of greater awareness. When we finished, he offered the following suggestions: be kind to yourself, do what is necessary to be healthy, be generous and kind to Lisa, protect yourself from negative thoughts and negative people, look for the good in things and be aware of all that is around you and all that is happening within you. Things will change. Simple words and simple advice from a man I trusted deeply.

Al and I kept in close contact and after a bit of time and counseling I took my first steps forward when I began to read again. Talking with friends or family was still too difficult, however books were a safe source of new voices. I had been on a path of study for a long time, and it had been a great intellectual adventure. Now it was personal. I needed my studies to be accompanied by an emotional investment that was far more meaningful and demanding. It is one thing to be a third-party reader; it is quite another to be a first-party subject. Al had asked that I return to some books we had read together in the past, and so I did. This time the pages were much more vivid, painted with references that spoke directly to my profound sense of loss.

Fortunately, the privacy of reading and writing provided a safe place to be vulnerable and expose my greatest fears and weaknesses. The metaphor of riding a bicycle is instructive. Although counterintuitive, when balance is lost, one must turn toward the fall in order to regain balance. In just such a manner, when a person is consumed with fear, anger, anxiety, or sadness, he or she must turn toward these emotions, expose their roots, and face them head-on to allow for the prospect of resolution and the possibility of recovered balance.

Should we turn away, the power of these tormentors only grows, as does our pain and suffering.

By opening myself up and probing honestly and deeply, I had the chance to regain my balance. As I took direct aim at my most pressing feelings of vulnerability, my greatest fear was exposed: the loss of my identity. As I explored this thought, I was struck by a powerful recollection of a recurring nightmare from my youth. In this dream, I had died and was now a ghost-like figure, hovering in space, endlessly watching the world turn. I was no longer a part of the world, I was no longer connected, and I was certainly without identity. And that was exactly how I now felt. I had invested very heavily in a personal narrative rooted in strength and independence, and had relied on my well-developed instincts to identify risks and move to places of safety quickly. Now without a job and without the ability to pursue my training, I believed that everything that I used to define and measure myself was in question.

One of the very few good things about reaching a place of great decline is that you become, in some respects, very aware. I do not mean to suggest that you are clear thinking, balanced, or resourceful. I am simply suggesting that you are aware of your circumstance and possess some understanding of the serious consequences that potentially lie just beyond. As a result, you soon become aware of the simple, existential choice presented: wallow and wither, or change. If you are fortunate enough to summon the energy to change, you place yourself in a surprisingly interesting position. Now that old ways, old thoughts, and old habits have been thoroughly contaminated with the perception of failure, you find yourself in a position to explore the new—an extraordinary opportunity.

We are all prisoners of a lifetime of baggage, and the chance to truly lighten the load is rare. I assume that very few would willingly choose to visit such a place to sort through their lives, but should that be your lot, you hold the prospect for real change. Even in the most disadvantaged circumstances, there is advantage to be gained if you can remain open.

TRIAGE

I t is hard to focus when your mind is consumed with risk. So my first task was to ease my greatest fear, which was the fear for my health. I needed to develop a sense of health security before I could turn to the other interconnected issues that were consuming my thoughts and feelings.

After initial testing by the cardiologist, the answers to my problem were still unclear. The functional elements of my heart were all in good working condition, and there were no related problems that could be identified. Given the potential medical consequences associated with my condition, the doctor was obliged to offer his version of therapy: drugs, electroshock, and ablation. Each came with a list of side effects, risks, and uncertainty, along with questionable forecasts of durable success. None of this gave me any level of comfort. More importantly, I was incredibly uncomfortable with the patient messaging I was being offered.

On more than one occasion it was suggested that by selecting one of these therapeutic options I could return to my "normal" way of living—back to the routines, practices, and expectations that had presumably been my sources of happiness before my condition. The thoughtlessness of this proposition bothered me on so many levels. Wasn't it reasonable to assume that it was these very routines that were somewhat responsible for my current health condition? If the reasons for my health problems remained unclear, was it wise to mask the underlying cause of my condition by forcing my heart to perform in a normal manner through the use of drugs or procedures? And most importantly, just when incentives for change in diet, nutrition, exercise, behavior, and so forth were most compelling, was it wise to remove these incentives by restoring my "normal" self?

Dissatisfied with the options offered by conventional medicine and fortified by our positive experiences with alternative medicine, I chose a different path. Rather than forcing my body to adapt to my expectations through the use of drugs and medical procedures,

I tried to adapt to the changes that I sensed my body was advocating. And to accurately interpret these messages it was important that I was uncluttered by medicines and procedures geared to suppress symptoms rather than seek answers. This choice required that I take meaningful risks. And to manage those risks I needed to elevate my awareness of the subtle voices spoken by mind and body that were here to provide me with guidance and information about my constantly changing condition. I needed to be highly aware and sensitive to the early signs and symptoms that signaled sadness, stress, weakness, pain, anger, disappointment, etc. I needed to be aware of everything, and I needed to be sensitive to as many of the responses, patterns and interconnections that I could identify. And when armed with this information, I needed to apply various forms of behavior modification and therapies in the hope of discovering a more sustainable way of living a happy and healthy life.

I want to emphasize in no uncertain terms that this was my choice, not necessarily the right choice. What if instead the cardiologist had identified functional damage to my heart? What if I had other, complicating medical problems? What if I had not had a history of good physical condition? What if I needed to remain in a stressful job environment? I chose my own path because I had the time, energy, ability, willingness, and curiosity to try.

This new direction had plenty of risks and no specific roadmap, but don't mistake it for some random walk. There was a new sheriff in town dictating terms and giving orders. Any path chosen or direction taken first had to answer to my heart. And should my heart not approve, it could choose to register its disapproval in extremely harsh terms. It was my job to learn how to tune into my heart and respond to what it was saying.

What I learned very quickly was that all my physical, emotional and psychological problems led directly back to my heart. Anger, sadness or pessimism registered similar responses from my heart rate and rhythm, as did simple physical exertion. Everything was connected and nothing could be overlooked or under-estimated. Furthermore, time was not my ally. With the risks associated with my heart problem still largely unknown, sloth and delay could allow the problems to grow deeper roots, making remedy increasingly distant.

With my attention focused on the search for a new way forward, it was incumbent on me to develop a support structure. I needed voices and viewpoints that could challenge, coach, and support me in this endeavor. In this regard, I really lucked out. I assembled a group of alternative healthcare providers who were exceptional in their craft. I found a new naturopath who was a truly gifted healer and whose science-based background was well suited for my particular problems. She was medically qualified, a believer in naturopathic therapies, and an incredible acupuncturist. Additionally, she was the most amazing diagnostician I had ever met. This was a critical skill set to help me interpret my body's reactions to the physical and emotional choices I was making.

The naturopath could be considered the GP of the alternative healthcare world. Naturopathic medicine believes that a body in balance should be well suited to fight disease. Testing focuses less on the presenting disease and more on the overall health of the body. As imbalances are identified, the naturopath attempts correction through supplementation, nutrition, and behavior modification. With a remedy applied, the naturopath monitors the body's overall response, as well as the body's response to the identified problem. From my experiences, the range of diagnostics employed and causalities explored provided me with a sense of confidence and comfort.

I was also in the care of a chiropractor qualified in the practices of craniosacral therapy. I had met Dr. T. after failing to find the relief I needed from my monthly visits to a traditional chiropractor. As I mentioned earlier, I have been a member of a wonderful karate studio. In my first years, the classes were populated with enormous, highly skilled students who really liked to mix it up. Many of the students were regular attendees, and by the end of the month, we were all sufficiently banged, bruised, and bent over that most chose to visit the local chiropractor to get straightened out. The doctor was a really nice guy, but his arms were the size of tree trunks, and every time he put his hands on my head to adjust my neck, I had the distinct impression that he could end my life in a nanosecond. This gave me no comfort, but I continued my monthly visits because, at each month's end, my posture once again closely resembled the shape of an *L*.

At the end of one particularly cruel month, I made my first appointment with Dr. T., rocking my attractively curved karate spine. After a very short chiropractic inspection, he pronounced my back completely healthy. Then he started probing me with questions about life. Eventually, he centered on my work, identified a particular area of stress, and took me through an emotional survey of the circumstances. With his exam complete, he ended the session by offering me a psychological prescription for dealing with the issues and then asked me to walk around.

It is important to understand that, at the end of the month, getting off a table was no easy task. But this time, as soon as I landed on my feet, I knew that things had changed. The tightness was released and the pain was gone. After a little rest I was back in karate class and I didn't need to return to Dr. T. for several more months.

Dr. T. would become another valuable partner in my quest for good health. But more importantly, this was the first time I had experienced the close connection between emotional stress and physical pain, or mind and body. Before this I had assumed that therapy consisted of discrete pairings of specific problems with equally specific solutions. But now I knew that was not the case. With more experiences and more evidence I began to believe that any strategy for healing that failed to account for the physical as well as the psychological and emotional was in some important ways either incomplete or not durable. It is not my intention to be rigid. But it is my intention to make people aware that the sources of healing are far broader and more dynamic than is conventionally believed to be the case.

These two healers proved to be staples in my roster, but I experimented with many others across a broad spectrum of therapies. Over time, it was important that I learned to manage these different agents. First, there were the practical considerations of time and cost. But there is much more. With experience, I also realized that the constant visits were, in fact, quite suffocating. When health practitioners become a steady diet, it is easy to identify yourself as a sick person. In my experience, even the best and brightest have tendencies to over-diagnose and overschedule, and it is easy to find yourself on a slippery slope. I don't believe that I have ever left a doctor's office without someone trying to schedule my next appointment.

I found it necessary to manage my own cycles of care in order to gain a measure of distance that allowed room for true healing. Healthcare is a give and take between the doctor and patient. Sitting back and simply waiting for your doctor to fix the problem is not a smart strategy. The patient needs to understand the problem, the treatment and their responsibilities to further the process. Managing the pace of visits was important in order for me to observe responses and make adjustments that could help direct the process going forward.

Two additional allies worthy of mention are Nancy and Jerry, the owners of the karate studio I attend. I was forced to take a brief hiatus when my heart was particularly compromised, but as I began to feel more secure in my health prospects, I was able to make a gradual return. This was important because when my heart condition first surfaced, I had chosen to live in relative isolation. The act of rejoining a community was critically important for my repair.

One of the important aspects of the karate studio for me was its role as a safe haven. When I entered the studio, I escaped the world for the next hour, free from the judgments and stresses that haunted me in many parts of my life. This was a place where everyone was invested in the growth and development of all the other participants. It was a place where I felt at ease. I was fortunate that Nancy understood that the martial arts were much more than simply a form of self-defense. She appreciated the value of healing practices such as tai chi and qigong, and was anxious to share her knowledge with me. Although I had to learn to change the focus of my practice, I could stay connected to my physical self in a community that continued to welcome me despite my new limitations.

Safe connections are absolutely critical to the construction of happy, healthy lives. When referring to the notion of "safe connections," psychologists are not simply referring to being in the presence of others. Rather, they are referencing a deeper sense of connection that can best be described as reciprocity. It is the knowledge that one is not simply seen and heard; rather, there is a deeply held feeling that one knows that he or she has a place in another's heart and is considered in another's thoughts. Only with these conditions fulfilled are feelings of good mental health possible. My reconnection with this community was of vital importance in helping me reestablish feelings of secure connection.

With a support system in place, I had to adopt practices into my daily routine that helped to make healing a steady, reinforcing ritual. One should never rely solely on the physician or therapist. You should view yourself in partnership with your caregivers. The hours they spend with you periodically could never replace the endless time you spend in care of yourself. Building personal support systems and practices to supplement your healthcare is absolutely essential to creating lasting results.

Before discussing some of the healing practices I have chosen for myself, I need to establish some baseline principles of healing. The best way to start is with a quote from my conversations with Al: "True healing happens when we don't care about healing because attachments bring garbage." There are many useful interpretations of this thought. For our purposes, Al was cautioning against attaching ourselves to a particular health care strategy along with the expectation of a specific outcome. When we make such mental attachments we are unnecessarily limiting both the number of potential healing outcomes as well as the paths we are open to exploring to reach these potential outcomes. We are narrowing when we should be expanding our search for remedy. And when we adopt this posture, we lose awareness of the full range of possibilities that are available to help us find our way to better outcomes. When you are holding a hammer, everything seems to resemble a nail.

The human design is the most complex machine ever imagined. The human brain alone is estimated to be comprised of eighty-six billion neurons connected by one hundred trillion synapses. And many aspects of basic human functionality remain beyond our full understanding. It is reasonable to argue that what we do not know exceeds that which we know. Therefore, it would be somewhat presumptuous to believe that the application of any specific drug, procedure, or health practice would produce the specific result predicted. The spectrum and nuance of possible outcomes is unimaginable. Thus, the best intellectual and emotional posture to assume when engaging in the process of managing complex health problems is one that values curiosity, diligence, awareness, and learning rather than the simple application of advice, therapies, and drugs, accompanied by an expectation of outcome.

Expectations of outcome may even serve to sabotage the healing process by creating tunnel vision, obscuring your ability to interpret observations and respond. Healthcare, whether we are speaking of the physical or psychological, is a marathon. At best, we are simply observers of the most mysterious black box ever imagined, doing our best to gather context and clues for interpretation. Healthcare providers can offer great insights and information, but they require the constant, clear-minded vigilance of the patient in order to properly shape the course of therapy. It is the patient who is tasked with detecting and interpreting the subtle voices that are produced by our minds and bodies, providing the color, context, and detail that inform further action. Turning your attention away from outcomes and centering your attention on the process of healing can help clear the mind of expectations that serve to keep your mind focused exclusively on the cure.

With the absence of expectations, information is processed without bias, and awareness of nuance is unburdened by the narrow view. Therapeutic direction is engaged without prejudice, and the healing process is no longer hostage to the emotions attached to outcomes that are viewed as less than entirely successful. When we disentangle expectations from observations, information gains greater clarity and decision-making improves. Furthermore, without expectations, the potential for a broader spectrum of outcomes is introduced, making valuable therapeutic room for positive, unintended consequences.

As an example, I want to offer one of my early outcomes. With great intention, I have tried to improve the rate and rhythm of my heartbeat for the last several years, and there have been definite improvements. But the unintended consequences connected with my actions may ultimately prove of equal or greater worth to my health than simply achieving my initial goal.

For years prior to my current condition, the only issue that doctors were concerned with was my blood pressure. My tests consistently registered readings of 140 over 90, the highest readings allowed before drugs were typically administered. I had tried everything to remedy this problem, but all my efforts were met with little to no success. Then I began to apply the various supplements, practices and behavioral strategies intended to help my heart heal. And slowly but steadily my blood pressure readings changed. Now, for the past several years, they have consistently been measured in the area of 110 -115 over 70 - 75.

So, although my efforts have not yet "helped my heart heal" by restoring it to a normal rhythm, they did result in an entirely unexpected positive healing outcome - a return to healthy blood pressure readings. If my focus had remained narrow, I may have missed this benefit and then failed to continue with therapies and practices that have been the source of important benefits. I can also report that my wife has noticed a meaningful change in my disposition that has led to a more positive attitude and a much better relationship with my entire family. By not attaching myself to the specific outcome of a normal heartbeat and rhythm, I made room for other therapies that have led to unexpected outcomes. I continue to apply all my chosen practices without reservation as I continue my search for new ideas. It is my belief that the consistent application of these practices yielded the unintended positive outcomes described and may ultimately prove to be part of the answer to my long-term goals.

It is important to understand that when you choose a sound therapeutic practice, it may not produce the specific outcome intended, but it may provide unexpected benefits that have great value and may indirectly contribute to the solution desired. Such therapies should be continued with vigor rather than disposed of as failed ventures when some arbitrary benchmark fails to be realized. Good health may not always imply healing, and healing may not always imply good health. The job is infinitely complex, and creating a clear line of sight to solve a particular problem may not be possible.

The better approach is to constantly learn and collect sensible behaviors, to be aware of all changes, and to never fail to improvise and adapt. Broaden, don't narrow; observe, don't expect; learn, don't lament; and remain steadfast, don't falter. As Albert Einstein once said, "Not everything that counts can be counted and not everything that can be counted counts." Patience, perseverance, and a clear mind may be your greatest assets in this process. Release yourself from attachments, and give true healing a chance.

Within the context of these broad principles of healing, I would like to discuss some of the healing practices I have incorporated into my regular health routine. These are the practices that I have chosen to support the treatments, therapies, supplements and dietary instructions recommended and administered by my naturopath and my craniosacral therapist. There is one very important observation that I need to emphasize about employing any or all of the following practices. There is compelling logic and preliminary evidence in support of their therapeutic value, and each comes at no expense and no risk.

MORNING PAGES

Morning pages are a very easy discipline to explain, but they are a bit harder to execute. Soon after waking, you simply commit to writing three pages, without any regard to what you are writing. When you finish the three pages, you throw them away without reading them. There is absolutely no script, no right or wrong, no expectations whatsoever. It doesn't matter what you write. This exercise can be done anywhere: on the kitchen table, in bed, commuting on the train to work, and so forth. Interestingly, the practice addresses many areas of great psychological importance.

Although we are still in the early days of research into the subjects of dreaming, REM sleep, and circadian rhythms, the uniform suspicion is that they are critically important to our good health and overall mental acuity. Apparently, while sleeping, we actually reshape and process information stored in memory that is largely beyond our ability to interpret while we are either awake or active. The sleeping brain also has the ability to reorganize and reprioritize this newly processed information, assigning essential information to highly available memory while relegating those memories of little consequence to places rarely visited. Morning pages is an exercise that tries to help you tap into the important work done while you were sleeping, bringing those newly organized thoughts to your awareness.

All of us have struggled with memories just beyond our grasp or connecting the dots of unfinished thoughts, only to 'sleep on it' and find new answers. Think of morning pages as a process that makes the search and discovery of these connections part of a daily ritual. And if it is reasonable to postulate that our ability to think creatively and perceptively is linked to our ability to connect our most valued memories with meaningful observations and experiences, then it may also be reasonable to understand morning pages as a valuable tool to help each of us capitalize on our daily renewal of intellectual vitality. Not too shabby for ten minutes of daily discipline.

Originally, Al had suggested that I do the morning pages every day for thirty days. But I was finding them so productive that I continued for ninety days. On the occasions when I wrote without conscious thought, I was pleasantly surprised by the random thoughts that arose and the distinct feelings of unburdening and awareness that I enjoyed. Since then, I revisit the morning pages when I feel unsure of my next step.

When I refer to healing practices, you may be surprised that I count this among them. I take a very broad approach to healing because I am convinced of how little we all know. In my case, I believe that my heart health is as likely to come from improved psychological health, as it is to come from biological repair. We saw an example of this when Dr. T. helped repair my back by addressing emotional issues rather than physical concerns. The act of writing morning pages helps me gain greater insight and awareness into my overall condition, and it helps me expand the search for creative responses to these new observations. That is why I include this as a valuable tool in my healing process.

GROUNDING

Human beings are electrical beings. The flow of electrical signals through the human cellular structure is essential to support proper biological functioning. Cardiac rhythms, circadian rhythms, circulation, the nervous system, and the immune system all depend on the vital conduction of electrical information. Unfortunately, our cellular signaling systems and the biology that they are designed to support are subject to disruption from the increasingly toxic environment in which we live. Advocates for the practice of grounding believe that through direct contact with the surface of the earth we can repair some of the harm done to our systems due to these environmental factors, as well as improve our overall health.

The earth is an electromagnetic planet that carries a large negative electric charge at its surface. Supporters of grounding argue that by walking barefoot we can tap into this large source of free electrons and figuratively tune up our bioelectric systems. Grounding advocates remind us that for the majority of our existence human beings walked barefoot, living lives in constant contact with the surface of the earth. But in our modern existence, direct contact with the earth's surface is no longer a common occurrence. We live in urban settings and we wear rubber-soled shoes, both of which prevent the transfer of the earth's energy into our bodies. As a result, we are losing contact with one of our important sources of natural healing.

Grounding is part of the back to nature movement, which believes that improved health and wellbeing can be derived from increasing our contact with nature. From an idealistic point of view, it is easy to identify with the naturalist movement, but it is more than just hope and fantasy. All of us have experienced the extraordinary health benefits that come from a walk on the beach, the sun shining on our faces, breathing the cool mountain air or walking barefoot in a beautiful park. These feelings and benefits are real, and increasingly, research is being produced in support of the health benefits drawn from such activities.

Unfortunately, the research in support of grounding, as well as its numerous health claims still fall far short of that which is required of rigorous scientific study. My decision to incorporate this practice into my routine was more a matter of judgment rather than facts. I know how great I feel when I take a hike in the woods or a walk on the beach. And I know that when I fail to enjoy these types of activities for any reasonable period of time, I genuinely feel their absence. For me the relationship between feeling good and contact with nature is without question. And even in the absence of scientific proof, this idea is still worthy of personal experimentation.

I assume that it is obvious that the evolution of human beings coincided with and was influenced by the evolution of our natural environment. As a result, is seems logical to conclude that these two complex systems evolved with many interdependencies and common purposes. And just as I know that I have gained great benefit from increased exposure to nature, I also know that our natural environment has come under considerable assault from a growing number of food, air and water toxins. And although it is still a controversial subject, I am also concerned with our constant exposure to the electromagnetic radiation emitted from the incredible number of devices and conveniences that populate our modern lives. I don't know exactly how these pesticides, chemicals and devices interfere with our bodies, but I feel certain they do. And it is hard to feel confident that the producers of any of these products, or the coalitions organized to support them, will be forthcoming with any research that does not support their economic self-interests.

So my conclusion was simple. Either grounding eventually finds support in science or I benefit from some form of placebo effect. And should neither of those things occur, I simply reap the benefits of a practice that gets me outside and in touch with nature a bit more often. Because I must endure the cold winters of the northeast, I found it necessary to invest a small amount of money in a grounding mat that I place under my bare feet when circumstances prevent me from walking outside. I feel pretty good about the investment.

I can't defend whether or not this specific practice is contributing to my good health. But I can claim that I believe my health is improving and that this practice suits my general parameters of a good therapeutic direction: sound logic, little cost and do no harm.

MEDITATION AND MINDFULNESS

I continue to practice and grow as a meditator. This has proven to be a pivotal part of my progress toward better health. There are so many books, magazines, and lectures devoted to this subject that for me to opine would be nothing short of arrogance. But it has been critically important to my improved health, so I want to make some mention of it. Meditation can take many different forms, and they are all worthy. I ultimately settled on a strategy that has provided great comfort and joy and has definitely contributed to my better wellbeing.

After all of my study, the only truth that I know to be certain is that the biology related to my condition is extraordinarily complex. In response, I tried to develop a meditation practice that would actively enlist my complex biology to aid in finding a solution. When one practices meditation, the aim is to quiet the mind by employing great levels of concentration on a particular point of focus. The intended consequence of these efforts is to create a space where great rest and expansion of the mind are simultaneously possible. This simple exercise is actually quite difficult to execute, but should you succeed, the benefits have proven to be both wide-ranging and broadly accepted.

As my practice evolved, I migrated through some of the traditional awareness items of focus, such as breathing and mantras, until I settled on listening to recordings of the human heartbeat. The heartbeat is repetitive, similar to breathing, and I found it to be extremely soothing and life affirming. Consequently, I have found it relatively effortless to maintain higher levels of concentration. On the surface, it seems to be a worthy meditation device. However, in my case, there is an additional purpose. With my focus on the heartbeat, I am exposing my mind and heart to the subtleties and complexities of a normal heart rate and rhythm, allowing for the prospect of my biology to retrain itself and find its own solution. So far, I can't report a cure, but my overall heart health continues to improve. I believe that assigning attribution will always be difficult. The more important goal is to assemble as many positive behaviors as possible in the hope of achieving an overall healthier outcome.

ACUPRESSURE AND MASSAGE

B ecause the process of healing demands constant adaptation, I have recently begun a new daily ritual of acupressure and therapeutic massage. The results have been quite encouraging. I have always experienced great physical response from acupuncture therapy, but the results were short lived, and financially I was forced to limit my visits. Acupressure replaces the needles of acupuncture, with pressure applied on many of those same points, using your hands. Because of my frequent visits to acupuncturists, the points were very familiar. Supplementing my knowledge and experience with new literature on the subject of acupressure has made it relatively easy to learn and implement.

But I didn't stop there. In the course of all my therapeutic experimentation, I was also exposed to a great deal of massage therapy, Chinese massage, and reflexology. These techniques dovetail nicely with acupressure because they all essentially try to improve energy flow through the body by stimulating areas known as meridians. While relaxing in the evening, I use the time to stimulate the points that therapists have focused on to aid in my particular circumstance. To date, the results warrant continued commitment.

I continue to adjust the areas I work on based on my research and responses to therapy. The practice seems to be producing similar results to those I achieved from my visits to the different therapists. I am hopeful that the consistent application of this therapy will create more durable results than those I achieved in the past. The process has already been of great therapeutic value by consistently creating feelings of deep relaxation that have been very helpful with my sleep patterns. The way I see it, I have a great deal to gain and very little to lose with this latest health choice.

JOURNALING

Another particularly helpful exercise to which I have committed considerable time and energy is journaling. I was an avid reader of spiritual and theological texts throughout the 1990s. Then, around 2003, I met Al, and he turned me on to more unconventional, Eastern religious works. This proved to be great preparation for the roller-coaster ride of life changes that stretched from 2007 to 2011. As I crossed over to a less healthy emotional place, my reading list expanded to include psychology, biology, and philosophy. Importantly, I started keeping a record of everything I consumed. Whether reading a book or article, watching a thoughtful movie or television program, enrolling in a Coursera or edX class, talking with a valued friend or advisor, listening to a TED Talk or attending a lecture—at the conclusion of any activity, I recorded the important thoughts and messages into my journals.

I have often heard the question asked, "If your house were on fire, what would you look to protect?" For me, it is clear: family first, journals second. The process of building a personal credo through my journals remains a particularly powerful exercise. As I have transcribed, organized, and editorialized thoughts of great personal consequence, my view of myself has changed considerably. What was once a random walk informed by the common culture has become a carefully curated point of view, informed by authors, friends, and advisors of great personal consequence. Although I wish I had started the process a little earlier, these writings are the most complete record of my thoughts and feelings during this period of pain and recovery. They are an important source for reference when I am looking for specific answers, as well as a general source for personal renewal and peace.

CHARITABLE WORK

Perhaps the most important therapeutic practice was my return to charitable work. During my experiences with sadness and depression, my preoccupation with myself was relentless. In some respects, I had no room for anyone else. It was this constant self-attention that led to constant self-inspection, which suffocated any prospect of healing. I am not sure any of our self-images can withstand such review, but when compounded with low self-esteem and critical eyes, the prospect of healing becomes remote.

Service is the antidote to this entire posture of self. Once engaged, the self is relegated to the back seat, and others become the focus. The sense of relief one can acquire from a little less self-attention is liberating, offering the first prospect of healing. In the charitable domain, performance, appearance, and position are devalued and are replaced by new commodities of worth, such as attention, compassion, and commitment. Measurements commonly applied in our daily lives gain little traction, and a sense of worth for all parties can once again be restored. Many times in the past, I acted out of a sense of duty and responsibility to others, but now I realized that my engagement was a responsibility vital to caring for myself. The meaning and value of charity were much more profound than I originally understood.

There is considerable support for this line of reason in all of the great theological texts. Their calls for acts of compassion are amongst the most consistent and compelling documented messages advocating for a change in priority from the self to others. Humility in our relationship with the divine, compassion for others, and sacrifice are the central messages of countless theological works devoted to the construction of healthy, happy, and meaningful lives. If you choose to doubt them as powerful advocates for this purpose, then you must ask yourself why these messages have found their way to the cores of all the great texts and have retained their high priorities, despite the unyielding scrutiny of countless great thinkers over thousands of years? Isn't it possible that generations of sages understood that compassion is more than just a calling to help others? Maybe the act of compassion is necessary to help ourselves by addressing some of our most profound personal needs and weaknesses.

If we were to try to synthesize these spiritual instructions into a simple, straightforward message, we might recognize it as a call to service. Charitable work (service) is one of the great cures for all that fails us as individuals, groups, and societies. From a pragmatic point of view, if you think of service in terms of those who serve and those who benefit, then you are likely engaged for your own benefit, missing the entire point. However, when service is engaged with an impeccable spirit, without expectations of gain or outcome, all are nourished by our highest need for human connection.

In contrast with the many other vital relationships that fill our lives—such as those in which we engage with family, friends, and business associates—the service connection is entered without the burden and responsibility of the social contracts we choose to cosign. For example, the generous act of caring for your family involves many obligations that are, in fact, self-oriented. It would not be uncommon to have one's self-image wrapped up in the accomplishments of a spouse or child who benefited from your generous efforts. There is absolutely nothing wrong with this, but the motivation of self-interest remains part of the equation.

There are many other examples we could summon of rewarding charitable engagements that are burdened by social contracts. Think of a request for charitable donations of time or money at your place of employment. You may be completely sympathetic to the cause, but to entirely remove the notion of self-promotion is unrealistic. Or consider your obligations and desires to serve the needs or requests of your community or your place of worship. All wonderful and worthy, but separating the purely selfless act from the burden of the obligated act can sometimes be very difficult to do.

In the purely charitable experience, obligations simply do not exist. When engaged in without any trace of self-promotion, the charitable act becomes a purely selfless act, and the feeling is very different. The transformative power of this simple, voluntary commitment helps us to both approach the Buddhist aspiration of cultivating freedom from the prison of the ego as well as answer the fundamental call at the core of all the great theological texts to "love thy neighbor." As the spiritual texts guide, the charitable act not only asks us to turn toward compassion and selflessness, but also encourages us to do the hard work necessary to turn away from hate, violence, greed, and egotism, making the truly transcendent experience possible. In many respects, it is easy to understand the Golden Rule as the ultimate manifestation of the religious or spiritual experience.

As a result of returning to charitable works I quickly felt the benefits of reorienting my focus from myself to others, but that was just the beginning. My new perspective of the charitable experience has been instrumental in helping me shift my view of my true self. Charity was no longer an obligation and duty; now it was an essential source of nourishment and growth. My perspective of who I am and why I am has irreversibly changed and many of the burdens I carried in defense of my self-image have been relieved. This unburdening has tangibly changed my outlook and has been instrumental in helping me find many of the creative responses to the challenges I faced, including writing this book. Without this dimension in my life, none of my growth and repair would have been possible.

I was fortunate to find an exceptional outlet to pursue my interests. I became a tutor, teacher, and financial advisor at the Mercy Learning Center in Bridgeport, Connecticut. The Center takes care of 850 women annually from over fifty different countries, providing childcare, legal services, healthcare services, and all forms of social work. It is the best model of service to an at-need community I have ever seen. And as someone who has run and advised charitable organizations, the efficiency of cost relative to the levels of service and care provided is tremendous. Their motto, "Educate a woman…educate a family" is spot-on when you understand the dynamics of the community.

This is a really tough area, and the women live in some of the most difficult conditions imaginable. But if you visited this institution with its 850 students, 100 daycare children, 220 tutors, and 30 staff members roaming its modestly sized quarters, the only thing you would see is respectful behavior and smiles. Every day it reinforces the transformative power of compassion and provides abundant evidence of our ability to solve our most complex social problems. If these were the people holding the megaphones in our society, the messages of hope and change would have a great deal more credibility, and we would all be better for it.

The most important point to understand is that by actively engaging in the process of finding healthcare solutions to fit your problems, you are already gaining great therapeutic advantage. Some would argue that this advantage comes from reacquiring a sense of control, but I disagree. When you seek control, you are, in fact, trying to insulate yourself from change, and that is fundamentally unhealthy. Relentless, unyielding change is probably the only immutable reality that exists. And when dealing with the infinite complexity of the human body, change is actually fundamental to its design. Thus, words like "cure" are extremely misleading and can even serve to divert attention from where attention is deserved. The far more sustaining posture is one that welcomes, accepts, and adapts to change, rather than trying to manage it.

Change is neither good nor bad, but it is always worthy of your awareness. Because of the marathon nature of the healthcare challenge, it can be reasonably argued that your attitude and awareness is of greater long-term consequence than any specific healthcare solutions employed. Given the complexity of the human design, you soon come to terms with the fact that answers are rarely conclusive and always subject to change. The process is never-ending, and it is your consistent commitment that will ultimately determine the durable nature of your wellbeing. This is a process that requires education over opinion, curiosity over convention, energy over sloth, and responsibility over resignation. And with these qualities embraced comes the prospect of resilience, the cornerstone of lasting health.

SANDCASTLES

Underlying this entire thought process, behind all the calculated attempts to make sophisticated logic of my chosen paths of therapy, lay a single regulating factor: trust. Trust is the quality that invests all information gathered with a sense of value and substance. It adds authority and belief to all decisions made. Think of trust as our most precious commodity. It is our personal gold standard. It is a thing of extraordinary value, yet its value may be hard to measure. It is traded with caution but offered willingly when fair value is gained. It can be a definition of worth, but it is a worth measured by infinite measurements. It is how we value ourselves and how we value others. It is the closest thing we have to our identities.

Consider one simple example of the power of trust, the placebo effect. As a result of our trust in the possibility of a cure for a range of physical and mental problems, we are at times able to command our complex biology to create therapeutic change beyond the abilities of our most well financed pharmaceutical companies and their legions of gifted scientists. The placebo effect is a physiological response triggered by a conscious, psychological cue. In other words, our belief in a cure for, say, pain, anxiety, or depression, using a pill that contains no active pharmacological ingredients, can actually create a neurological response similar to, and at times better than, the response targeted by highly engineered drugs.

By definition, all placebos are inert. They do not contain any functional agents capable of creating a physiological change in a patient. So why have so many patients reported relief in clinical trials when given a placebo rather than an active drug? We know our minds and bodies are capable of releasing a range of agents that can ease pain, repair injury, fight infection and slow the progression of disease. But when a patient enrolls in a clinical trial, he has failed to find relief. So what changes when a patient takes a placebo that enables them to call upon their powerful biology to find relief or remedy?

The common answer to this question is belief. Belief in a cure or remedy is sufficient to call upon your body to heal what ails you. But that answer does not go deep enough. Imagine you walked into a hospital to participate in a clinical trial for chronic pain relief. The receptionist escorts you into the examination room and offers you a pamphlet that explains the basic science and the potential benefits of the drug you are about to receive. When you finish reading you are extremely optimistic. You begin to believe this pill may work. Then the door opens and the janitor walks in and gives you a pill. Are you still as enthusiastic about your prospects of a cure? If, on the other hand, you had been escorted into a doctor's office, with all of his or her credentials on display, would your initial belief gain increased credibility?

Now let's take this line of reasoning one step further. Think of the following exercise. You close your eyes, fold your arms across your chest and fall back into the arms of another. Belief is the feeling you have before you commit to the fall, trust is when you do it. As we will soon discuss, trust is all about risk-taking and belief does not require risk. When you take risk, there is a commitment that touches your heart, mind and body. Trust is palatable, trust is powerful and trust resonates deeply. The placebo works because we trust the doctor. And our trust makes us willing to take risk and commit. It is that commitment that fulfills the necessary and sufficient conditions to change beliefs and expectations into something that resembles a cure. Trust can transform the potential of a placebo into a catalyst for biological actions of consequence.

I am not here to argue conclusive scientific truths. But the observation that trust may be an engine of extraordinary healing is certainly worthy of further study. If the placebo pill is measurably nothing and the effect is measurably something, why wouldn't we want to investigate further? Unfortunately, we all know the answer to that question. With little prospect for profits, research efforts lack the traditional incentives. However, for our purposes, the incentives are clear. The ability to connect trust with powerful, biological consequences should be more than sufficient to galvanize further interest in this transformative subject.

The power of trust has influence far beyond our biology. Trust is an incredibly important agent that sits at the center of all the decisions we make. The veto power with which it is invested can corrupt hours of hard work spent, large sums of money expended, and networks of support and advice gathered. But trust is not simply some naysayer bringing clouds to the picnic. Trust also has the ability to convert thoughts and actions into answers and convictions. It has the power to summon energy, create alliances, and construct lasting beliefs that are the engines of our lives. Trust is our unified expression of our thoughts and feelings that ultimately translate into the risks we choose to avoid and the rewards we choose to chase.

What all of this implies is that I can calculate and cogitate all I want about my healthcare choices. Unless

I come to choices that I trust, my ability to sustain a healthcare regimen that will prove both durable and effective is highly questionable. Without trust, we inevitably lapse, undermine, and disregard the strategies and structure necessary to give any path of remedy a reasonable shot at success. And of equal importance, with trust absent, we may fail to enlist the full support of our complex biology necessary to maximize the benefits of our chosen courses of therapy.

To infuse this subject with added consequence, one need only consider the fact that trust is amongst the most fragile commodities in our possession. Think of how difficult and time-consuming it is to earn trust, yet how fast and easily it is lost. Leading lives reliant on healthy relationships with trust can feel as if we are perched on the narrowest of balance beams, trying to find our way to safe ground. It is without wonder that we often find ourselves with feelings of stress and anxiety. Our entire lives are carefully intertwined with this fragile commodity, yet few, if any, are aware of the central position it commands. If we are to be active actors in our lives, we must better understand how we manage our relationship with this incredibly valuable asset.

PART 3

REINFORCEMENTS

I t's astonishing that the study of trust has not gained
wider visibility. Our elections are largely decided
based on trust. Legal verdicts, police actions, and military engagements are all matters of trust. Even the of-
ficial motto of the United States was changed in 1957
from *E Pluribus Unum* ("One from Many") to "In God We
Trust." Using the word "trust" was no accident. There
are many other ways to express our reverence, devotion,
and love of God. But in this case, we chose to endow and
endorse the power of God through our trust. Further
endorsement of the power of this word is evident if we
examine our money where the same phrase "IN GOD
WE TRUST" is written across the back of our notes and
coins. The calculated use of the word *trust*—not faith,

not belief, not devotion—was clearly determined to be of critical importance to gain the requisite authority. Trust is both a powerful force of nature and a powerful message.

"Trust" is one of the most commonly used words in the English language. Yet, from my experience, its application to matters of great importance is often an afterthought. I have never been to a business meeting that defined, monitored, or measured its progress in terms of trust. I have never borne witness to a product, program, or policy that began with trust and then worked backward to designs, plans, or strategies. The only people and organizations that seem to understand the central importance of trust are in the fields of advertising, marketing, public relations, and politics. And they are largely in the business of manipulating trust rather than nurturing it. For them, it's a commodity; for the rest of us, it should be gold. Unfortunately, very few seem to understand this reality. The promoters and marketers see trust as the reward; the rest of us see it as a byproduct of some other reward.

Trust is also our most important gatekeeper. The people, affiliations, communities of interest, and institutions we associate with are those with which we share trust. Those not part of the inner circle are granted much less access to all that we have to offer. In many cases, trust is intentionally withheld from those unaffiliated. How common is it for a Democrat or Republican, black, white, or brown, straight or gay, citizen or foreigner, to withhold their trust from one another, making open and honest dialogue virtually impossible? As a result, trust acts as a powerful filter of information, ideas, and knowledge, impacting our views and perspectives. As we narrow our scope, we narrow our willingness to accommodate difference, making connection more difficult. By regulating our power to connect, trust regulates our power to empathize. By regulating our empathy, trust regulates our humanity.

I know with absolute certainty that trust has been amongst the most influential variables governing the direction of my life. The more I process, the more I believe that my relationship with trust was at the center of the personal struggles I suffered during my adult life. Trust was at the heart of many of my difficulties in business, it is the root of my consistently pessimistic view of the future, and it is the reason I am so willing to isolate when trouble arises. All of this translated into a generally negative point of view that has been incredibly corrosive to my overall health and happiness. Conversely, evidence of the extraordinary value I place on trust is abundant—the best example of which is the unshakable bond I share with my wife, predicated first and foremost on trust. I don't suffer because I fail to understand the value of trust. I suffer because I guard its value far too closely. I don't believe I am alone in this regard.

THE ANATOMY OF TRUST

The French philosopher Jean-Paul Sartre argued that we are the products of our choices. I would like to start with this thought and dissect its construction, in search of its fundamental relationship with the concept of trust.

It is very hard to make separate any part of our being that is not defined by choice. If one chose to challenge this assumption, one could cleverly point to the involuntary systems in our bodies charged with regulating many of our vital functions, such as heartbeat and digestion. Certainly these systems function without choice? Yet the choices we make in the care and feeding of our minds and bodies greatly impact the quality of their functioning. Indirectly, then they are subject to choice.

Next, one might challenge the assumption by examining the broad scope of study that tries to understand and analyze thoughts attributed to that which is beyond our conscious awareness. Although these preconscious thoughts are potentially constructed without choice, there exists ample evidence in support of a different conclusion. Both the conscious and preconscious fundamentally function by exploring the interplay of memories, observations, and patterns. Where, when, and how this information surfaces in part determines which of the two categories it is assigned.

Conscious thoughts are more closely aligned with deliberative, calculated, and measured reasoning, while preconscious thoughts are more likely characterized as reflexive, intuitive, and spontaneous. The difference between conscious and preconscious thoughts is that the patterns analyzed may be drawn from different sources, the observations selected from different pools of available experience and the memories recalled from different stores of information. But the fact that the preconscious draws from memory suggests that it is tied to past experiences and past decisions. Thus, we can deduce that the preconscious is also indirectly a product of our prior conscious choices.

What remains is the subject of conscious thought. Conscious thought is generally considered a matter of awareness of self and other. It can be further defined as our ability to sense, feel, or be awake. But thinking of our selves as nothing more than awareness seems to fall far short of the notion of identity intended by Sartre. How we choose to process and apply observations and information that enters our orbit of awareness would seem to draw us much closer to any reasonable definition of self. We are cognitive beings, we are physical beings, and we are emotional beings. If we believe that the theory of evolution is a sophisticated system of design, then it would be logical to assume that our functionality was organized with clear purpose. The product of purpose is inevitably some form of action, and action is ultimately a function of choice.

Are you all that you know or are you that which you do with the knowledge you have acquired? Are you defined by your disabilities or how you function in spite of them? Are you defined by your abilities or what you choose to do with them? Are you physically gifted if you never use your muscles? Are you an actor because you have memorized the lines? Are we static or dynamic beings? The answer is clear. We are what we do, and to do is to choose.

We are what we choose.

One choice I am truly proud of was how I handled my health problem. This was certainly not a path of my choosing, but when dealt this hand, I used it to expand my life, not make it less desirable. I was always a rather simple sort. I loved my work, I loved my family and close friends, and I loved my physical fitness. I never missed a day. One or two hours of daily grind made me feel empowered, youthful, and confident. I had no sense of boundaries in the present or the imaginable future. When my health problem surfaced, a large part of my identity and daily activity was neatly cleaved from my body and soul. For a while, I was lost. But, in this particular case, I surprised myself. Rather than abandon the activities in disgust, I learned the value of moderation. I accepted a new vision of my physical self and learned to participate without regret and with great joy. Choice was fundamental to my changing identity.

Having created a linkage between choice and identity, it is now important to understand that which impacts choice. At the center of choice reside two questions: what are the risks and what are the rewards? These are the two universal questions that permeate all facets of choice. When we consider choices of great consequence, it can be easy to frame the application of risk and reward. But these two subjects also play roles in all the inconsequential decisions that consume our lives.

Consider something as simple as looking in the refrigerator to choose between blueberries or strawberries to grace your morning bowl of cereal. It is hard to associate more than a fleeting thought with this choice, but, in fact, you go through the same motions as you would with the more significant decisions of your life. So how do you choose? Which is the freshest? Which looks like it will taste best? Which goes best with your cereal choice? Is there risk? Sure there is. The wrong choice could potentially ruin your breakfast. Is there reward? The right choice could make your breakfast satisfying and delicious.

It sounds ridiculous, but it's not. All choice is an active process. If we wish to choose, we must act, and actions come with consequences, great and small. Because this particular action comes with such little risk and reward, the choice barely registers in our consciousness. But the important point is that the risk-reward equation is a fundamental part of all our choices.

Our choices are determined by the way we process risk and reward.

To understand risk requires that we understand our fundamental human design. The notion that all beings are predisposed to survive and persevere is intuitively obvious. And it should be just as obvious that, in order for that to happen, we must put our interests before others. But what is less obvious is that in order to protect our self-interests, we have acquired a powerful negativity bias that meaningfully changes the way we evaluate risk and reward. To provide an example of negativity bias I want to turn to the behavior of sharks.

I love to scuba dive. As is common with most inexperienced divers, I studied the predatory habits of sharks before my first dive. What I learned surprised me. Apparently, most shark bites do not end in fatalities. Soon after taking hold of a person's leg, a shark commonly releases and swims away. The reason for this is straightforward. We are sizable and unfamiliar, and they cannot risk injury from prey they don't understand. Injury in nature is almost always fatal. Thus, their brains instantly process the risk-reward and choose to give up the certain reward of an unfamiliar meal for the uncertain risk of finding their next meal. The sharks are fundamentally encoded to proceed with an abundance of caution.

For many years, human beings lived in similar circumstances to those of our predatory analogs, reinforcing the dire consequences of negative outcomes. Accordingly, evolution made sure that our minds and bodies were highly sensitive to many different sources of negative information. We process negative data quicker than positive information. We experience a cascade of physical and psychological reactions in response to negative inputs versus little response to positive inputs. Our attention to negative news is much greater; our dreams are, on balance, more negative; and we use negative language references far more frequently than positive references. We pick up negative body and facial cues more easily, and negative memories are far more durable than their positive counterparts. All of this is testimony to the fact that negative experiences receive far greater priority in memory than do positive experiences. And with greater priority comes greater access, increasing the influence negative memories have on how we experience the world and how we respond to the world.

The logic behind this design is straightforward. Our negativity bias is designed to ensure that we stay alert to any and all signs of danger and move quickly to keep ourselves safe. In broader, simpler terms, our negativity bias is hard wired into our basic design to keep our undivided attention squarely trained on the subject of risk.

We are intrinsically wired to focus on risk.

To explore this subject further I want to look at the subject of survival from a different perspective. You can think of our human system as a reservoir of resources. We have intellectual and physical requirements that call upon our stores of energy to power the business of our lives. Thinking, acting, and emoting are all consumers of our limited resources. Which resources we choose to deploy and at what cost are the basic decisions that define our existence. It is not the presence of these resources, but the choices of when, where, and how we use them, that gives voice to our beings.

The question of resource allocation drills down to the core of our human nature. In a big-picture, evolutionary way, it is what races through the lion's mind when it is deciding whether to chase the antelope. You may dismiss this thought process as simply pure animal instinct, but in fact you would be very wrong. When you take the time to analyze this decision process, the first thing you realize is that it is far from simple. And after accounting for the ramifications of these decisions, the complexity makes perfect sense.

Consider the geometry involved. Prey is located at some distance and, if approached, is likely to move at some predicted speed and set of possible angles based on topology and known animal behavior. The lion must consider the size and speed of the prey, ambient temperature, and the predicted length of the chase, and then there must be some equally complex calculus of the physical costs to the lion itself. Muscle exertion, internal temperature regulation, hydration, compensation for injury, and threat of injury must all be considered. All of this must be quickly calculated relative to the internal resources at the lion's disposal. The animal must have an instinctive appreciation of the rewards of success and, more importantly, the risks of failure.

Risk and reward permeate all aspects of decision-making associated with resource allocation, but they are far from equal partners. Let's continue to use the example of the lion hunting for food to explore the asymmetrical priority assigned to these two fixtures of choice. We start with two assumptions. First, a lion has the physical wherewithal to complete four hunts. Second, if a hunt is successful, the meal provides the lion with the physical assets needed to complete four additional hunts. Now let's examine how risk and reward change with success.

If the lion were to begin with a series of successful hunts, in our very simplistic exercise, its physical capacity to go on additional hunts would increase from 4 hunts to 8 to 12 to 16. Clearly the prospects for our lion are very promising. But a different view of these same numbers may offer new perspective into how success may alter our lion's behavior.

With its first successful hunt the lion increases its physical resources by 100 percent. But as the successes continue to accumulate, the rate of growth of its physical resources actually begins to decline from 100 percent to 50 percent growth then followed by 33 percent growth. In other words, the worth to the lion of each additional success declines in value. This is an example of the law of diminishing returns. The law is used to describe a point at which the benefits gained from an action or process fail to sufficiently compensate for the energy or effort required. And this is not just a discussion of math. This is also a discussion of motivation, incentives, and of course, risk and reward.

Just imagine you are homeless and someone hands you $100. The impact on your life is enormous. If this generosity were to continue on a daily basis, eventually the value of the $100 would begin to lose its impact after your most important needs are met. In a similar manner, the lion will likely lose its motivation to take additional risks or seek additional rewards until its resources become less plentiful, again making risk-taking acceptable and rewards worth pursuing. What this suggests is that after some number of successes, even though there may still be a high likelihood of further success, the lion may choose to simply rest.

Now let's examine the math of failure. If our lion begins with a failed first hunt, its store of resources would decline by 25 percent. And if the lion's efforts were to continue to fall short, the second failure would cost the animal 33 percent of its remaining resources, followed by a third failure costing 50 percent of available resources, and a fourth failure which would likely end in death.

The consequences of failure compound in a far different and alarming manner than do the benefits of success. And it is this basic mathematical reality that alters judgment and changes decisions. For the successful lion, decision-making continues to be governed by something we would consider to be rational or reasonable because risk and reward remain somewhat equal partners. For the unsuccessful lion, decision-making is quickly compromised and choice can longer afford the luxury of balance. Fear and desperation soon become all-consuming subjects and choices normally considered far too risky are now given serious consideration.

There is one additional factor that is worthy of mention to complete our picture. The lion is not some machine that features a convenient on-and-off switch. Whether active or at rest, the animal's physical systems continuously consume its precious personal resources. Time is not its ally. Eventually it must act, even if the circumstances are less than ideal. Accordingly, with each passing moment, the risk profile of our lion leans further in the direction of increasing risk.

This is the great catch-22 of failure. When you try to catch up, you likely choose risks that make you fall further behind. Risk is insidious. It creates enormous emotional, intellectual and physical challenges that distort decisions and change our futures. Simply stated, the costs of failure are debilitating, and the lion's margin for error quickly disappears with each misstep. Statistically, it is in the best interest of the lion to keep a carefully trained eye on the risks of failure, rather than focus on the potential rewards of success.

When the lion chooses to act, it intuitively accounts for the fact that life penalizes failure much more aggressively than it rewards success. As a result, it must process choice to account for this reality, surveying opportunities with an eye for clear advantage. There is a cost and fragility attached to life that demands our careful and undivided attention to risk. If survival is the ultimate endurance contest, then we must accept that endurance is a matter of overcoming failure and duress, not celebrating success. If we are to endure, if we are to survive, we must train our attention squarely on the subject of risk to construct a platform that puts us in position to selectively pursue success.

We choose based on how we process risk.

To briefly summarize, our identities are defined by the choices we make. And the choices we make are defined by our attitudes and responses to risk. Thus, our identities are intimately tied to our dispositions toward risk-taking.

THE NEW CURRENCY

Although we no longer hunt to survive, survival is still a worthy challenge, and the new currency of survival is money. Money is the means by which we satisfy our basic needs for food, clothing, shelter, and water. And if money is now our new currency for survival, then we should expect that when money is the subject of discussion, our negative risk-based biases should dominate our thought processes.

Consider the thought process underlying a meaningful investment in the stock market. If a person were to make an investment, there is the possibility of great reward that could satisfy important needs for safety and security or possibly fulfill desires for luxuries that have been postponed. Now imagine this same person considering this same meaningful investment with the added responsibilities of a family to care for, rising healthcare costs, a demanding job with an uneven profile of job security, and a large mortgage to pay. Without any special understanding of the risks, rewards, and timing of the investment, should you go for it or keep your cash safe? If you are like most, you fear the consequences of failure more than you desire the rewards of success. This is a rather straightforward, simplistic example, but it still serves to show the balance of obligations (risks) that most of us must process when making financial choices of consequence.

In the clear light of day, our negative biases make complete sense. These are the biases we all carry when purchasing new homes, buying cars, changing jobs, or moving to new towns. The terms and conditions we need to negotiate are radically different from those of our ancestors, but the life-altering consequences of poor financial decisions are largely the same. Our ability to provide the equivalent of food, clothing, shelter, and water for our families can quickly come into question. To accommodate our fundamental needs, we are programmed to embed negative experience with enormous content, making these memories easily found and quickly accessed.

Evidence of the way we organize and store negative information is available if we study the strategies employed by people who train to compete in memory competitions. Professional memory competitions are a thing, and training is serious business. Importantly, memory development is not only about IQ. There is considerable strategy and practice required. To improve their ability to memorize particular targets, the competitors create relationships and attachments, making the targets rich in available associations. The more sensory information, contextual information, and linkages created, the easier it is to access the objects in memory. This systematic addition of bulk to memories is similar to the process we undertake when we store our negative thoughts and experiences in memory. We are instinctively inclined to embed and enrich this information with as much content as possible. With more content comes more neurologic pathways, making negative information more easily accessed. With this information accessible, we are brought closer to choices that avoid risk and keep us safe.

If I think about my experiences as an investor, a similar pattern appears. The information embedded in negative experience is far richer than that ascribed to positive experiences. Reward is generally relegated to the status of an afterthought. In the stock market, success is often tagged with moments of great joy but very little else; there is no self-reflection, rumination, or careful examination of cause and effect. Conversely, losses are emotionally very draining and are often accompanied by anger, physical outbursts, self-doubt, sadness, fact checking, and endless review. This examination can last for weeks, in contrast with the recollections of the successes, which fade quickly.

Sadly, I can say unequivocally that when I recall my two greatest successes in the stock market, the first thoughts that resurface are those that reflect on the additional profit not captured rather than the life-transforming profits gained. Positive memories seem to sit quietly while negative experiences, as well as those experiences perceived to be negative, become rich in content and context and shout from the rooftops. Our system of storing memories is extremely invested in making sure that negative information is easily accessed in the hope of steering us clear of poor outcomes in the future. And when negative information can be connected with the subject of survival, our associations, access and attention is consuming. Therefore, it is perfectly logical, in the context of our modern financial existence, that matters of money are accorded the greatest priority in our thoughts and memories to help us navigate the risks that threaten our survival. Money is the currency of our survival.

Further evidence of the power of negative experience comes when I re-experience negatively charged memories. Oftentimes, my body and mind tend to react like I was revisiting a minor trauma. Should a sound, sight, or smell trigger some particularly sensitized memory, I am instantly subject to many of the same physiological and psychological details with which the memory was encoded. Increased heart rate, chills, sweating, panic, anger, self-doubt, and sadness are not uncommon. I also notice how difficult it is to stop my mind from revisiting these negative images over and over. It is a rare moment when such strong feelings accompany a recollection of a positive memory.

The situation actually becomes more difficult when I make efforts to purge or suppress these difficult-to-experience thoughts from memory. By doing so, I effectively increase the potency of the negative memory rather than achieving the intended goal of eliminating it from thought. Ironically, the more often negative events are repressed, the more emotion that is attached, creating more connections, more triggers, and, in the end, more powerful memories. Our negative experiential bias is powerful and self-reinforcing. It changes the way we interact with the world.

We have quickly navigated a simple logic tree that followed a single thread of reasoning from our identities to our choices and from our choices to our negative biases and eventually to our relationship with risk. Now I want to take this line of reasoning one step further. When a person chooses to offer to another his or her trust, the person is engaged in the most comprehensive human expression of risk taking.

To trust is to take risk because it is a choice that makes you vulnerable to another person or thing. The decision to trust includes the evaluation of such factors as integrity, ability, strength, and surety. But it goes far beyond conscious choice. It taxes our intuitive judgments, it calls upon our reservoirs of related experience, it gives voice to our evolved histories of acquired knowledge, and it calls upon that which is beyond rational judgment to address such questions as hope, belief, and faith. It calls upon all we know, all we believe, and all that we feel to determine whether to attach ourselves to this person or thing to help us achieve that, which is currently beyond our grasp.

Consider the opposite of trust: control. By definition, trust is the act of surrendering our personal power to another, as opposed to control, which is the act of exercising our personal power over another. In other words, trust is about risk taking and control is about risk avoidance. Control is our effort to fulfill our needs or desires to make known that which is not knowable. Trust asks me to accept the unknown. When I say, "I love you," I am willing to accept that you may not offer your love in return. In the case of control, you may never offer your love until the other chooses to take the risk first. Trust asks us to turn toward risk and respond to the unexpected. Control asks us to turn away from risk and hope that the unexpected does not happen. In our simple example, the trusting person embraces the unknown with a sense of wonder, while the controlling person turns away from the unknown in return for the measured response. The difference speaks to everything we aspire to and value. It changes every risk we take and every decision we make. It changes how we wish to engage the world and what we hope to achieve for our time on this planet. To know trust is to leave control behind.

When we trust physicians, we believe they can guide us to health. When we trust teachers, we hope they can guide us to new knowledge. When we trust leaders, we expect that they will provide us with safe and secure futures. When we trust friends or spouses, we hope that they will offer us secure connections. When we trust, we are taking risks that ask us to draw upon all that we have experienced and all that we have learned, both now and in generations past, to answer the questions that are of the greatest consequence to all that we hope to achieve in the future.

When we ultimately pair our commitments to act with our assessments and acceptance of risk, we are engaged in acts of trust. To trust requires that we have taken risks. To have taken risks demands that we have acted. And to have acted requires that we have made choices. Therefore, to choose is to trust. We are what we trust. Trust is our ultimate expression of how we synthesize all we know and all that we don't, all that is raised to our consciousness and all that remains just beyond our reach. It is our most intimate and comprehensive expression of what we choose and, in that regard, it is our most accurate expression of who we are and how we interact with the world.

When I speak of self, when I speak of identity, I am speaking of whom I choose to trust and what I choose to trust. We are who and what we trust.

THE DEEPER DIVE

Identity, trust and choice are all joined at the hip with our dispositions and attitudes toward risk. To move our discussion forward, we must dissect this powerful subject further.

First, we need to understand that risk is a matter of personal perception. Risk is not retrospective, but prospective. It is not about loss, but rather about the fear of potential loss. Think for a moment. Is it more difficult hearing the bad news from a doctor or waiting several weeks for test results before the doctor can deliver the news? Once the uncertainty becomes certain the fear begins to recede.

In finance, risk is a calculation of probability. For example, what is the chance of not finding a green ball hidden beneath one of six possible shells? In life, risk is not purely a calculation. Risk requires context, risk requires personal investment, and risk requires fear of loss. Does a billionaire fear losing one million dollars? To the rest of us, this loss would be devastating, but for the billionaire, it is insignificant. No fear. Does a healthy teenage boy fear losing his healthcare? The rational adult knows how fragile health can be. For the indestructible teenage boy, health is a certainty. Does a Buddhist monk fear losing his worldly possessions? If the monk does not value his possessions, then there is no personal risk of losing them. No fear, no uncertainty, no risk.

Risk is dynamic, because that which we view as threatening changes with circumstance and time. Primitive man was primarily concerned with the physical dangers that threatened survival. But now, what threatens survival is far different. We no longer kill to eat; we purchase what we eat. We no longer build our shelters; we buy and rent them. We no longer gather materials to build fire; we turn on the electricity. Money is now our currency of survival, and the infinite connections that impact our ability to acquire and lose this valuable resource have redefined the ways that we define threats.

Consider this bizarre connection. A factory worker in Iowa receives an alert on his smartphone that the stock of his parent company in New York has been halted from further trading. Just imagine the range of threats that now circulate through his mind: layoffs, college tuition, mortgage payments, healthcare coverage, and the health of the Iowa economy. Just twenty years ago, this was unimaginable, and now we know that this only begins to tell the story of our interconnected lives. Threats can come at any time, and survival is very much in the balance.

Risk is relative and risk is elemental. Risk gives definition to those things of greatest personal meaning and consequence. Risk is primitive. It connects us with that which we fear and that which threatens our survival. Risk is a fundamental part of human nature. If the presence of risk depresses our willingness to pursue opportunity, is it possible to imagine that the absence of risk welcomes opportunity? If the presence of risk darkens mood, attitude, and disposition, does its absence lighten disposition? If the presence of risk puts your body on alert, does its absence offer the potential for calmness and acceptance? Risk is intrinsic to our human design. It is a powerful, internal barometer that regulates behavior and influences choice.

The most interesting thing about risk is that you actually feel it. You feel it because risk is not just an intellectual and emotional exercise but a biological exercise as well. Risk is always present, but it manifests psychologically and physiologically based on a broad spectrum of factors. At one end of the spectrum are those things of little personal consequence and meaning that register little response. But as the fear of consequences grows, so does the depth and range of biological responses. Finally, when uncertainty is introduced to subjects of great personal meaning and consequence, we feel threatened. And when we sense threat, a cascade of biochemical and electrochemical activity is launched, preparing our bodies to respond. The nervous system, the circulatory system, and the endocrine system are instantly enlisted, sending and receiving messages to and from all the vital organs of the body, preparing them to act and preparing them to perform.

When threat is perceived, blood pressure rises, heart rate quickens, energy increases, muscles tense, temperatures rise, and respiratory rate accelerates, all in preparation to act. As a result, your mood changes; you are more focused and vigilant. You have access to memories typically out of reach. The most subtle facial expressions, smells, intentions, intonations, and movements are now accessible. Muscles and reflexes operate with extraordinary strength and agility, and decisions are constructed with speed and conviction. As muscles tense, your posture changes, and your face conveys the impression of intensity and focus. And as you become more focused your gaze steadies, and any trace of a smile or welcoming appearance vanishes. Your sweat glands release perspiration, and you may even start to shake, all offering clear indications of your changing disposition and intentions.

Without conscious thought or awareness, in the blink of an eye, your body and mind are changing. You are ready. But the question is: ready for what? Catching a hard-hit baseball down the third base line? Returning an overhead smash in a grueling tennis match? Confronting a bully? Avoiding a car that suddenly swerves into your lane? Giving a speech before a packed crowd? Buying or selling a stock, when stock prices are tumbling? Breaking up with your girlfriend? Taking a test in school? Losing a job? Buying a house? The list is endless. Your ancient biology has sensed uncertainty, braced for unfamiliarity, and readied you for threat. You are primed to deal with risk.

The blizzard of scientific language that is used to describe our biochemical and electrochemical responses to risk is extremely dense. It would include a discussion of the electrochemical signals that traverse the complex fabric of our cellular biology. It would cover the complex cocktail of hormones that pulse through every vessel of our bodies, up regulating and down regulating activity to optimize muscle and organ performance. But understanding these details is not our mission.

We are more interested in identifying and understanding the forces that join to alter choice, risk, and trust. And once armed with this knowledge, we can elevate awareness and discuss strategies to improve our ability to respond.

For our purposes, there are two important points regarding our biological responses to risk that require our attention. First, our response to risk is a highly evolved, complex process that offers unique insights quite separate from those of the rational mind. With the support of highly charged senses and incredible levels of focus, we are provided with sources of information about our internal conditions and external environments that are not available under normal circumstances. And this preconscious thought process comes with its own unique language to convey its valuable messages. The conscious mind communicates using logic and reason, structures that I would characterize as prose. The preconscious mind communicates through emotions, feelings, and instincts, structures more closely associated with poetry.

Often it is easy to dismiss these preconscious sources of information as simply noise and distraction, but to do so would be unwise. Their existence in and of themselves is worthy proof of the fundamental importance they play in our successes and survival. If this were not the case, then evolution would long ago have eliminated these substantial calls on our precious stores of personal resources. Our human design would simply not be sustainable if elemental functions cost our system $100 worth of resources to produce $1 of resource-driven insights. And all of us are fully aware of the costs we suffer managing the preconscious poetry of our feelings and emotions.

Consider the example of walking alone in the woods. It's an experience you highly value, but you are aware that this activity comes with a certain amount of risk. As a result, your body and mind adjust to higher levels of awareness. Out of the corner of your eye you spy a shadow. For some reason, it seems out of place. You may or may not consciously recall the article you read three weeks earlier about an increased number of bear sightings, but some part of you surely remembers. One possible device your body may choose to employ to gain your attention is to create the sensation of butterflies in your stomach. This is not some random reaction; this is part of a sophisticated, early-warning system often referred to as a stress response.

By definition, stress is neither good nor bad. It is simply the result of your complex biology releasing hormones and diverting blood flow, preparing your muscles and organs for action. Time will tell whether your elevated state of awareness justified the use of the resources deployed by your body. The psychic rewards gained by the walk were well worth the effort and resources expended. But it may also be worthwhile to appreciate the subtle changes you instinctively incorporated into your walk in an effort to keep yourself safe. Your sophisticated internal biology made an incalculable number of adjustments, sharpening awareness and energizing muscles in order to optimize your ability to respond to threats.

The second observation worthy of our attention is the impact our risk-response machinery has on our conscious thoughts. Not only are these preconscious thoughts constructed separately from our conscious thoughts, but they are also constructed before our conscious thoughts are organized. As a result, they have enormous influence over the conscious thoughts that follow. Whether we choose to run from the shadow or continue at the same pace, the walk is no longer the same. We are now invested in a heightened level of risk. Until we reach a safe space, our conscious decision-making must carry the burden of our preconscious awareness. The length of our walk, the directions we choose, and the terrains we select are now all infused with preconscious bias. Whether we are aware of the presence of our preconscious thoughts or appreciate the risks they call us to attend, we must understand that our freedom to choose is no longer the same. Our preconscious awareness of risk has now altered our landscape of conscious decision-making.

Our biological responses to risk set in motion a series of physiological and psychological changes that create the framework within which our conscious mind can begin its intellectual proceedings. Consider the following circumstance: a person approaches from behind and places his or her hand on your shoulder. How might you respond? Is it a threat or an opportunity? Is it a beautiful woman wishing to make your acquaintance, or is it the jealous husband of a beautiful woman, angered at her affectionate preoccupation with a stranger? What we don't know is how this will end. What we do know is how it will begin. Before you have a chance to think, before you even turn around, your biology will have set in motion a series of changes that will alter your disposition and influence your initial response.

Do you remain relaxed, turn, smile, and open yourself to experience? Or do you recoil in fear, acquire a menacing glare, and adopt a defensive posture? Research has proven that that which you choose can have considerable bearing on what happens next. Smiles generally make you appear more attractive and change the moods of those around you. Smiling can lower the heart rate, reduce blood pressure, and actually signal the release of biochemical agents that lift mood, brighten outlook, and improve connection. Quite different from the biological response one might associate with a menacing glare. Which one you adopt will have a lot to do with how things end. But the important point to understand is that how you initially respond is not a matter of choice.

Our responses to uncertainty are products of our experiences, memories, and current conditions. Are you riding a winning streak, feeling very self-assured and confident, or have you been experiencing difficult times and feeling a bit down? Have you recently been given the phone number of a beautiful woman at a bar or have you recently been the victim of a violent crime? You bring a lot of baggage to every new experience, and with that baggage comes a lot of bias. So when confronted with the unfamiliar or the uncertain, your biology effectively confirms your predisposition and amplifies its direction. If, when you turn, your predisposition happens to suit the circumstances, your chances of success increase. But if that is not the case, you begin your next engagement at great disadvantage.

Preconscious bias changes your disposition toward uncertainty and therefore your appraisal of risk. For example, if you recently invested in ten stocks and they were all profitable, I would imagine that your predisposition toward the next risk would be considerably different than if your prior ten investments were all losers. Whether you choose to invest or not has far less to do with the merits and risks of the next investment and far more to do with your appetite for taking the next risk. Objectively, we could argue that this makes little sense. But we don't live in objective realities. We live in subjective realities. And the subject of that reality resides within. Our predispositions meaningfully influence the risks we take and the decisions we make. The preconscious offers the menu from which the conscious gets to choose.

Think of your predisposition as your in-house attorney. The attorney's job is not necessarily to find the truth but rather to find answers to the questions of their choosing. So if you're a bit beaten down and are looking at a prospective investment, you might choose to frame the decision in somewhat unreasonable terms. "I will only buy this stock if it can double in the next twelve months with very little risk." Alternatively, if you have been on a real winning streak, you may frame the decision quite differently, making the investment easier to accept.

Our predisposition effectively frames the decision in terms that are compatible with our desire to take risks. By changing the hurdle rates a decision must navigate, our predisposition changes the conditions attached to the questions of the moment. If a particular risk is framed in such a manner that it is always unacceptable, does the analysis that follows really matter?

Our predispositions are part of our preconscious machinery, communicating with us through the less direct paths of emotions and feelings. The biases and biology that conspire to form our preconscious thoughts craft the questions of our choosing. By choosing the questions, the preconscious regulates our definitions of acceptable risk, which limits both our choices and our willingness to trust.

Nowadays, our in-house attorneys seem to be working overtime. The new ways that we conceptualize survival and the factors that impact this new interpretation of survival are so nuanced, so complex, and so dynamic, that threats appear to be more numerous and more present than ever. We live in a constant state of information overload, and uncertainty is now a certainty. Past patterns are under siege, and stability has become an unaffordable luxury. Given our new circumstances, it would not be surprising to believe that our dispositions are becoming increasingly defensive, our hurdle rates are rising, and risks appear to be less and less attractive.

If this is true, does negative bias gain added authority? Does risk morph from uncertainty to threat? Do our negative predispositions become entrenched? And with increasing negative bias, does stress migrate toward chronic stress? Do the questions asked by our in-house attorneys become too difficult to answer? Do choice and trust lose the agile posture that offers us the best prospects for health, happiness, and success?

Our perceptions of risk alter our biology, our biology amplifies highly available memory, available memory biases observed experiences, experiences bias perceptions, and perceptions alter choice and trust. The intersection of preconscious poetry and conscious prose creates cycles of behavior that change our predispositions toward risk. Choice is not the product of a dispassionate and deliberate analysis, as we believe it to be. It is more the product of the intersection of highly available, negatively biased memory and biased interpretations of observed experiences that are registered with our in-house attorneys to construct the questions of our choosing.

The subtle voices of preconscious thought detected through our feelings and emotions need to be understood as unique and important sources of knowledge, capable of both informing and biasing conscious thought. With greater awareness of these sources of bias, we improve our ability to compensate for the factors that conspire to construct the questions that are far to easy for our conscious mind to reject. If we can recalibrate the scales of our preconscious thought to account for the increasing levels of uncertainty and unfamiliarity we experience, we may be able to reclaim our freedom to choose, as well as our freedom to trust others. And if we are capable of becoming great curators of our biases, we may eventually acquire the freedom to choose well and trust appropriately.

MIRACLES

Sometimes, to gain insight into a subject, it can be useful to consider the extreme, the outliers that challenge convention. Fortunately, when examining the subject of trust through the lens of one of its surrogates, belief, little effort is required to find worthy examples. Through books, magazines, the Internet, nightly news, personal knowledge, historical reference, legends, poems, and traditions, we are all aware of countless tales of inexplicable healing, medical mysteries, and stories of extreme survival. Central to many of these tales is the subject of belief.

Despite many attempts to dissect and diagnose the conditions and circumstances of these unusual cases, their unique and random nature will always keep them distant from the requirements of scientific validation. Only the existences of these individuals and their stories remain as powerful testimonies to the possibilities of belief. And that is more than sufficient to move our inquiry forward because our curiosity is not captured by the stories themselves, rather it is held by our interest in the power of belief. Deeply held belief is simply not possible without trust, and trust is what we wish to better understand. Trust in the messages, trust in the messengers, and trust in that which is beyond rational conclusion are the essential foundations of all beliefs.

Using religious belief as a proxy for examining trust sheds enormous insight into our subject of interest. When you consider the entire spectrum of benefits that accompany religious belief, you quickly gain appreciation of its incredible potential as a tool for promoting psychological and physiological health, healing and general wellbeing.

Religious life is all about connection. Congregation, collective prayer, group song, and community rituals create a social experience, a support structure, and a sense of community that satisfies our fundamental need for safe and secure connections. And this is no small matter, because it is safe and secure connections that form the bedrock of our sense of personal agency. Our sense of personal agency refers to those feelings of competence and confidence that enable us to take the actions and make the decisions that can influence the direction of our lives. A sense of personal agency is the foundation of our psychological stability, it is the heart of our resilience and it is the basis for our willingness to connect with others and take risks. The access to a community where all are respected, all are valued, and all voices are heard is far different than the competitive cacophony that dominates our lives. And it is just such an environment that nourishes the prospect of a strong sense of personal agency.

If we next look beyond the potential benefits attributable to a strong sense of community and support, and consider the benefits associated with belief in the sacred, the power of the religious experience grows. Belief in God is the simplest path to a less self-biased existence. The call for humility and the command to love one's neighbors gains considerable momentum when one makes a commitment to obey an all-powerful being. And by following these simple and central messages, belief in God reinforces our participation in the connected experience. However, the benefits go far beyond simply reinforcing the connected experience. When a person enters into a sincere relationship with God they are rewarded with an extraordinary gift. In exchange for our commitment of compassion and good works, the believer is given the gift of control. Questions normally beyond reach are given a framework for understanding. And with this knowledge, the believer acquires feelings of security and conviction that endow him or her with hope and optimism when both would normally seem to be distant.

If any of us were privileged to participate in an activity or belief system, that offered safety, support, connection, and control, we should expect the cascade of psychological benefits to be of substantial consequence. It does not require an advanced degree to appreciate that less feelings of social isolation translate into less fear and less anxiety. And less fear and anxiety eases our perceptions of risk. And when we are not overwhelmed by the presence of risk, our feelings of stress recede. And if we can possibly link participation in a community of belief with feelings of less isolation, fear, anxiety, risk and stress, then we have come upon an observation of great consequence. Because if and when feelings of social isolation migrate to sustained feelings of social isolation, then stress migrates to chronic stress, and when that happens everything changes.

A stressor is anything that disrupts our homeostatic balance. The stress response is the biological responses that are initiated to gets us through the stressor and then return our biologic systems back to a state of healthy balance. Stress is normal, stress is healthy and stress can even be fun, for short periods of time. But when stress is persistent or chronic, it can be life threatening. And that is a condition that more are suffering with greater frequency as the terms and conditions of our modern struggle for survival continue to change.

The health consequences of sustained stress are many. Studies have linked chronic stress to heart disease, depression, diabetes, and dementia. But these are only the first derivative consequences. Chronic stress is also extremely harmful to our immune system. And when our immune system is compromised, so is our ability to fight all forms of disease, injuries and infections. As a result of this connection to the immune system, chronic stress can be linked with any and all the of health conditions we suffer.

However, the health consequences only begin the discussion of the effects of chronic stress. It not only changes our moods and dispositions, but it also makes it easier for us to acquire fear associations and hold on to them. Chronic stress makes us more impulsive, more negatively biased and more reliant on habitual actions - behaviors that lead us to be more self-oriented, more fearful and less empathetic. And as we increasingly withdraw and protect, we become increasingly isolated and as a result experience more stress. The presence of stress is actually highly predictive of our perceptions of future stress. Thus stress is actually a precondition for more stress.

Chronic stress also damages many aspects of our cognitive functioning. It impairs working memory and makes it more difficult for us to acquire and synthesize new information. And as we become further removed from awareness and objective observations of our environment, our ability to properly appraise and process risk loses critical balance and decision-making suffers. Chronic stress damages our health, damages our judgment and is a gateway to more stress. It can't get much worse than that.

The feelings of connection that accompany a strong sense of community are the perfect antidotes for our rapidly growing experiences of social isolation and chronic stress. In fact, the AARP foundation has recently characterized social isolation as a rapidly growing *epidemic*. Predictably, numerous studies have documented the comprehensive health benefits that accompany safe and secure connections. Our cardiovascular, endocrine, autonomic nervous and immune systems all accrue important and lasting benefits from these favorable social circumstances. And if longevity can be considered a worthy proxy for overall health, then it should come as no surprise that several meta-studies have convincingly demonstrated that the risks of all-cause mortality decline substantially for those who benefit from strong social connections.

And the benefits grow if we consider the sense of control acquired when one enjoys a personal relationship with God. A strong sense of control can impact a person's perception of circumstance. A person of strong belief is less likely to fear uncertainty because uncertainty does not necessarily exist. When in alliance with the all-powerful, the belief in a plan and a purpose offers the prospects of motivation, confidence, and conviction that compel action rather than easily concede defeat. People of belief are more likely to reshape risk into challenge, adopt optimism when dealing with the unknown, and summon resilience in the face of unexpected difficulty.

No doubt many of us can reframe these advantages into disadvantages. Trepidation versus assurance can be a valuable asset when dealing with threat. A healthy appreciation of uncertainty versus conviction can increase risk aversion when risk should be avoided. And if self-confidence leads to action when either the action or the self-confidence is misplaced, poor outcomes likely follow.

Alternatively, is self-confidence a worthy asset when tempered by the humility that is demanded when entering a relationship with God? In what circumstances is advantage gained by pessimism versus optimism? When is it better to look backward rather than forward? When is it better to stay down when visited by misfortune rather than to rise back up? Who is more likely to benefit from the power of the placebo effect: the person of faith or the person without faith?

People of belief benefit from a broad spectrum of advantages gained from their participation in a supportive community and their connection to God. When confronted with tragedy, emergencies, or crises, it may be reasonable to believe that the benefits derived from strong support and connection may endow a person of faith with important psychological and physiological advantages. It may be reasonable to believe that a person benefitting from these important advantages is more optimistic and confident than the average person and therefore is more likely to stay engaged when others begin to shut down. It may be reasonable to believe that a confident and optimistic person suffers less fear, anxiety and stress. It may be reasonable to believe that a person who is less stressed burns fewer personal resources and is physiologically better positioned to meet short-term challenges. It may be reasonable to believe that a person who is suffering less stress is better positioned to explore options and process risk. It may be reasonable to believe that a person in possession of these advantages might make better decisions. When all of this is taken into consideration, it may be reasonable to believe that extraordinary stories of cure, healing, and survival are not impossible to believe at all.

The larger point I wish to offer is that belief and secure connection offer the prospect of a virtuous cycle of benefits. Better overall health begets a greater sense of agency, which begets better decisions, which begets better health. And on and on we go until, unexpectedly, miracles appear, when in fact they were never miracles at all. Maybe they were the far less romantic products of an advantaged psychological profile that led to certain biological advantages which improved the prospect for better decision-making.

Religious participation and belief in God offer compelling examples of the power of trust. They are also powerful reminders of the attributes and conditions we should strive to acquire and experience to empower our lives outside this singular lifestyle choice.

Questions of belief in God and participation in religious ritual have preoccupied a considerable amount of my intellectual time and energy. Unfortunately, there seems to be little relationship between the effort expended and the clarity gained. I have never come close to a feeling of belief, and the rituals have never provided a sense of comfort or a source of identity. Although the passion of the religious experience has escaped my grasp, my study of religion and belief has provided me with meaningful perspectives that have helped me live a healthier life.

I offer the following dialogue to sum up my personal perspective on the subjects of belief and religious practice.

If God exists, I would hope that He or She would be willing to talk. And when I ask His or Her thoughts on religious practice, I imagine that He or She would reply, "Religion is something humans created to give them a source of comfort when comfort is hard to find."

I would remark that religion and religious practice have been the source of a great many wonderful things and what seems to be an equivalent number of dark things.

God would then reply, "When people use religion to make certain that which is not, to make tangible that which is not, to give definition to that which cannot be defined, and to create boundaries to that which is boundless, unfortunate things happen."

I would then ask, "What, then, is your message? What is it that you offer us?"

God would reply, "Choice. When you feel angry, choose love. When you feel hatred, choose compassion. When you feel selfish, choose charity. When you use force, try to heal. When it is dark, look for signs of light. When you stumble, choose to pick yourself up. When others stumble, choose to help them get back up."

In my opinion, God's gift is choice, and man's burden is God's gift. It is entirely up to each of us to use God's gift wisely. We have the power to choose, and if we do so wisely, we have the power to live happy and healthy lives.

Belief seems to have played an important role in the development of humanity for thousands of years. Is it possible to argue that it is part of our evolved human nature? Is it something we can learn to access even if we don't share in the sacred experience? I don't know. But I believe that it provides powerful evidence of the important role trust can play in our lives. Trust can be a catalyst for some of the truly transformative powers we experience individually and as members of our larger affiliations. Any loss of our capacity to trust should be considered a great threat to our survival.

DYNAMIC TENSION

Earlier in our discussion we defended the idea that our identities are closely linked with our choices. We then described the central role that risk plays in guiding our choices. And lastly, we described trust as the most comprehensive expression of our willingness to take risks. We used this logic to argue that trust is central to our identities. I now wish to argue that trust is not only a matter central to our sense of self, but is also a matter central to our existence. Trust is fundamental to our existence because our survival is dependent on connection, and secure connection does not exist without trust. Exploring the linkage between trust and survival through the next few sections will offer guidance into the complexities we must navigate to find a place where the prospect for healthy trust can be restored.

In order to thoughtfully discuss trust, we must revisit the subject of bias. We have already discussed negative bias. But there is another source of bias that requires our attention; self-bias also plays an important role in shaping our realities. The theory of natural selection is all about advancing the self. It is a fundamental component of the evolutionary competition for survival that requires each being to consider them selves before considering another. However, in our contemporary culture, understanding the self has become an incredibly complex affair. Before we can pursue strategies that promote ourselves, we need to invest meaningful time and effort into framing our personalized views of ourselves. And without a comprehensive understanding of who we are, how can we possibly be capable of advancing our wants and needs?

We are no longer cavemen with a limited worldview. Our complex lives and equally complex world call upon us to develop highly sophisticated and nuanced views of ourselves. We now see ourselves through lenses that span an incredible spectrum of lives led. We have identities as single adults, married adults, fathers and mothers, children and grandchildren, athletes, businesspeople, caregivers, social beings, sexual beings, political thinkers, educated adults, socially conscious members of society, and citizens of the world. Can you even begin to fathom when or how this list might arrive at a place of reasonable closure? What we now mean by the term "survival" is certainly considerably more complex than the understanding held by our predecessors, whose list may have begun and ended with provider, protector, and procreator.

The cultivation of self-image is one of the great projects we engage in throughout the course of our lives. Understanding who we are informs what we must do—in the broader, modern sense—to survive. But there are insidious consequences associated with this project. The world is dynamic, and the pace of change seems to be constantly accelerating. Unfortunately, with the passing of time, our self-images become increasingly static, rooted in the past, where the vast abundance of information that informed their creation exists. It's simply a matter of math. As we age, the volume of information already acquired, defining who we are, increasingly overwhelms the incremental information yet to be acquired. As we attempt to retrofit our increasingly static self-images to suit an environment subject to constant change, we fall prey to unyielding sources of internal conflict.

Being self-biased creatures, we are reluctant to accommodate this tension. In response, just as we invested significant time and energy cultivating our self-images, we now channel similar energy and intensity in defense of our great creations. As we continuously invest and defend, it is logical to believe that the barriers we construct to protect our self-images make it increasingly difficult to gain a clear, unfiltered perspective of the changing realities we experience. Over the course of time, these barriers become so well fortified that they act to undermine their intended purposes. Rather than serve as a protective shield, they increasingly shield us from an accurate view of the present. As a result, we become increasingly exposed to inaccurate information and vulnerable to the consequences of the poor decisions that inevitably follow.

The self-bias and negative-bias models that were once charged with keeping us safe in our primitive world must now share a more complicated stage with the cooperative models that dominate our modern social and business worlds. Networks may now be more predictive of success than individual achievement. Geography is no longer a limiting factor. And a landscape of increasing change is now part of the status quo. A personal narrative of stability is no longer an option. Ever-increasing premiums are being placed on relationships and cooperative work environments to manage the increasing levels of complexity and the accelerating pace of change. The terms and conditions of our survival are changing, and our need to connect is more important than ever. And that means that trust now commands center stage.

Not surprisingly, evolution is well aware of our need to connect. Our brains have tripled in size over the past two million years and much of this growth was devoted to expanding our capacities to cooperatively plan, communicate and problem solve. In other words, our brains have grown in size to improve our capacities to connect. Our larger brains came with many benefits, but also many costs. Childbirth became more physically costly. The time required for children to develop both physically and mentally grew longer. And because our large brains are disproportionately large consumers of energy, we required more frequent feedings.

To improve our odds for survival we needed to develop more cooperative living strategies to satisfy our changing requirements for food gathering, child rearing and protection. To incentivize this behavior, adaptations evolved to support our need for strong social bonding. Our sophisticated brains, nervous system and complex supporting biochemistry evolved to help us interpret and anticipate the actions and intentions of others. And these abilities and understandings facilitated cooperative behavior that fostered environments that afforded us the time needed to develop and gain long-term advantages from our newly developed mental machinery.

There are many worthy examples of how our biology has evolved to encourage and help us gain advantage from our sophisticated capacity to connect. One obvious example is our sense of touch. Touch is fundamental to how we experience the world. Touch is the first language between mother and child, and numerous studies have proven the incredible developmental growth that accompanies its presence, as well as the mental, emotional and physical challenges that come with its absence. Many have experienced the important role touch can play in healing by reducing stress, lowering blood pressure, slowing heart rates and fortifying our immune systems. And we have all enjoyed the experiences when touch stimulated the release of hormones that catalyzed the emotions of love and attachment. Our human sexuality and tribal bonding are dependent on touch. Handshakes, hugs, kisses, chest-bumps and high fives are all examples of touch that cement alliances and mobilize actions that change our lives. It does not require a great leap of faith to understand that touch is integral to strong connection and cooperative behavior, both of which are fundamental to our health, happiness and success.

Relatively recent discoveries have upped the ante in support of our biological need to connect. From an evolutionary perspective, we are witness to the pivotal role empathy plays in driving the biologic urges of parental care and nurturing. With the discovery of mirror neurons, it is possible to speculate on our biological connection to our empathetic instincts. When we see someone expressing a range of emotions—for example, sadness—cells called mirror neurons fire, seemingly enabling us to experience the same sadness. If early scientific claims prove to be true, that mirror neurons can empower a person to embody the emotional pain and suffering of another, then mirror neurons could be considered an important fundamental feature of our ability to construct strong and secure social connections. Many different areas of the brain, as well as specific hormones, have been connected with the complex emotional and cognitive functionality that drives our empathetic abilities. Mirror neurons offer additional evidence of the depth to which our biology has adapted to accommodate and facilitate human connection.

But there is more. Neuroscientists have discovered that social pain (feelings of rejection, isolation, and inferiority) activate the same regions of the brain as physical pain. Our bodies actually experience a similar pain response to both the physical and the emotional. Furthermore, the same brain circuits activate, whether one is the subject of the social pain or is simply responding empathetically to another person's pain. Thus, physical pain, social pain, and empathetic pain all share similar neurological pathways. This is very important from an evolutionary perspective because things that cause us pain are considered threats to our existence. Therefore, if empathetic pain is ascribed a similar biologic logic as physical pain, then, from an evolutionary perspective, empathetic pain can be considered a matter of survival.

If empathy is biologically linked to survival, then it is possible to biologically link connection with survival. And if connection is dependent on trust, then we have created our first linkage between trust and survival.

If we choose to align ourselves with this logic, then it would be reasonable to surmise that we were not only designed to encourage human connection, but we were also designed to make human connection one of our highest priorities. Just as our biology requires priority for the self, it also demands priority of the other. This is our burden of dynamic tension.

THE CONTEMPORARY
CONUNDRUM

The shared priorities of self-bias and group connection have been in place for thousands of years. Our success as a species would suggest that we have capably negotiated this balance over time. But it is my observation that evolutionary time is under extreme time-compression stressors. And now with the rise of the social media experience, many of the biological and psychological skills we have developed to evaluate risk, choice, and trust are under assault.

How do we compensate for an online relationship that does not allow for taste, touch, and smell? What is lost when body language and vocal tones are largely absent? How do we adjust for the loss of visual cues, gestures, and expressions, some of which are so subtle that we have yet to fully understand their functions? How do we compensate for connections that are predicated on highly skewed imagery and messages that are not subject to context and inspection? If one looks at our new environment from a very broad perspective, it may be reasonable to interpret that we may have chosen to accept a bargain that exchanges more human contact for less human context. And in that exchange, what is gained may pale relative to all that is lost.

We are the most connected society to have ever lived. Over a quarter of the world's population have active social media accounts. Yet in 2017 the World Health Organization updated its fact sheet and listed depression as the leading cause of global disability, affecting more than 300 million people worldwide. The report goes on to say that close to 800 thousand die due to suicide each year, and that suicide is the second leading cause of death amongst 15-29 year-olds. Ascribing attribution to support this anomaly of more connection accompanied by greater depression would not be difficult. The debate regarding this subject is broad and highly engaged. In the context of our discussion, I would like to offer the following observations.

When we substitute face-to-face experience with our technology-intermediated experiences, we lose a large portion of the highly complex sensory information that has evolved to help us create secure social connection. These are the cues we have long relied upon to judge intentions, attitudes, and feelings. Without these valuable inputs we are less capable of empathy, less willing to take risks and ultimately, less willing to offer our trust.

The basis for community, the foundation of shared values, and the sense of common humanity all require meaningful, empathetic connection to establish durable platforms for trust. When rich connection is absent, it becomes far more convenient to objectify, demonize, and divide in the service of self-bias. From this posture evolves fear, loneliness, isolation, anger, depression, and at its worst, hatred. This is the danger we must contemplate when we swap rich, face-to-face connections for easily constructed, highly curated, comfortably distant, digital connections.

In the digital setting, we rarely feel vulnerable, and we are removed from the consequences of our words and actions. In short, we lose integral elements of the human experience. The digital experience is not inherently negative. The problem surfaces when it proves to be a satisfying substitute for real, human connection. In time, social skills erode, self-bias grows, and trust suffers. We become less human and see others through these same eyes.

Our capacity to trust is sourced from our intellect, from our physicality, from our experiences, and from our evolved nature. It is not predictable, formulaic, or easily subject to academic models of behavior. I anticipate that our technological attempts to create adequate substitutes for all that is missing from rich, person-to-person connection will fall far short of what is required. And as our reliance on technology grows, our capacity to trust may continue to decline and suffer.

For me, trust is more closely aligned with the agile stance rather than the scripted response. It is a disposition or attitude that leads with inquiry rather than answers. To develop our capacity to trust, we need to exercise our trust muscles. In neurology, there is a concept called neuroplasticity. Simply stated, it references the mind's ability to adapt. Consider the incredible sensory acuity achieved by those who lose their hearing or sight. Their remaining senses become far stronger to compensate for those lost. The brain has an amazing ability to reorganize, and the changes made gain strength and resilience through repetition. That which you practice grows stronger.

If we wish to maintain or possibly advance our capacity to trust and be trusted, we must develop exercises to support our changing needs. We must cultivate exercises that value and engage our empathetic instincts. We must seek exercises that promote a healthy balance between self-bias and the connected experience. We must elevate our awareness of our negative biases and expose them to the rigorous review of our conscious beings. We must start new conversations, create new alliances, and launch ourselves in new directions in the hope of finding a remedy to one of our most destabilizing problems. In a world where the fundamental is change, the best posture is one that values awareness, effort, intellect, and agility. These are the qualities that fortify trust.

If we approach the problem by trying to assess whom to trust, what to trust, and when to trust, we become nothing more than a dog in search of its tail. The more sustaining strategy would be to turn the focus inward. If we can become aware of the biases and accompanying subtle biology that influence choice, we can make efforts to restore the balance required to properly address risk and choice, and then possibly restore our capacity to trust.

We have discussed very briefly the dependence of choice on both conscious and preconscious thought. We have also looked at negative-bias and self-bias and the counterbalance offered by our need to connect. When all is operating properly, risk is evaluated with a reasonable level of clarity, and trust benefits from a healthy balance of self-interest and connection. But these are far from normal times, and our vital sense of balance is at risk. It is imperative that we actively seek out strategies and behaviors that can change the odds.

SEARCHING FOR REMEDY

I want to start with charity. We have already covered this topic, but I want to emphasize its importance as well as approach it in the context of our discussion of trust.

Charity is a direct counterpunch to the disconnected experience. By closing distance with those less familiar, we begin the process of reclaiming our capacity for empathetic response. Distance promotes difference, difference is unfamiliar, and the unfamiliar catalyzes our risk response, making connection more difficult. When I speak of difference, I am not referencing those attributes and qualities that make us unique and give life special meaning. I am referencing those most basic elements of our humanity: shape, features, size, color, smell, language, posture, and so forth, which can signal risk and conspire to disrupt our empathetic engagement. Proximity is the only path to fundamentally challenge these patterns and reframe our definitions of difference.

Our elementary design is infinitely wise. But it would not be unreasonable to believe that our ability to evolve and adapt are confronting challenges we are ill-equipped to manage. We now live in a world shaped by technological timeframes, artificial intelligence, automation, and global perspectives. The word "continuity" is now more closely aligned with notions of impediment, while our most celebrated technological changes are now referred to as disruptive. Time is no longer an ally as our subtle biology seeks to retain its evolved purpose and identity. To aid in this time of transition, we must put all options on the table. We must look within to elevate our awareness and cull the biases that conspire to reflexively categorize the unfamiliar as too risky. Simultaneously, we must develop new skills and practices that restore, revitalize, and reaffirm our capacity to connect. Trust lies in the balance.

Charity is an effective pathway by which we can actively exercise our empathetic muscles and retrain our fundamental biases. Charity is the antidote to the social media experience when connection is far less than skin deep and relationships last no longer than the time it takes to read 140 characters or admire a carefully curated photograph. In the charitable experience, distance and difference are given notice, and we are asked to call upon our complete arsenal of sensory, emotional, and intellectual weapons. Our entire empathetic superstructure is forced to participate in a demanding workout. With our empathetic muscles stretched and our defenses disarmed, our relationship with risk is challenged. We are asked to connect with the unfamiliar. We must overcome bias to fulfill obligation. Charity questions the preconscious assumptions that underlie our relationship with risk and therefore our ability to offer our trust. Empathy opens doors. Charity asks you to walk through them.

The other advantage of the charitable experience is the reorientation of our personal gyroscopes, creating new reference points of other versus self. In a world that has neutered our capacity to connect by failing to enlist our five senses, the charitable experience turbocharges its engagement. When interaction demands levels of attention and compassion far beyond normal social engagement, our empathetic response is powerful. And if this could become part of a lifestyle or a ritual, the balance we seem to have lost can be reacquired with plenty of room to spare.

It is important to recall that connection is not just a psychological benefit. It is also accompanied by powerful biological benefits, benefits that multiply when accompanied by the feelings of compassion and gratitude that are part of the charitable experience. It is certainly reasonable to hypothesize that the powerful feelings of connection acquired through religious participation may also be possible through compassionate, selfless acts of charity. The connection to God may be absent, but the strong sense that one is taking part in compassionate actions that form the essence of God's message may go a long way toward bridging the outstanding spiritual gaps.

I believe that a regular diet of charitable experiences offers the potential to fundamentally change the shape and content of our deeply held self-images. The charitable experience begins with a focus on others. It values different qualities and attributes than those admired in our regular lives. It inescapably challenges who we are, what we are, and where we are. It can be sufficiently jarring to allow new ideas, messages, and perspectives to gain traction among the entrenched self-images that definc our lives. With our deepest held beliefs challenged, we introduce the possibility of reshaping the context of many of our held biases. With bias challenged, it is possible to imagine the prospect of a better profile for decision-making and an improved capacity to trust. Consistent charitable experience has the power to reshape our lives.

If we could muster an institutional effort that would facilitate physical, face-to-face, regular charitable experiences in all of our lives, the fundamental change in our communities, in our places of work, in our society, and in our policies would be transformative. When we restore connection, we resuscitate the capacity to trust. When we restore trust, we fundamentally alter the way we evaluate risk and choice. When we improve choice, we can begin to imagine the prospect of real and durable change.

PREGNANT PAUSE

Given the tools at my disposal and my regular commitment to charitable activities, I must ask: Why am I still so far from a place I hope to be? What does it take to convert knowledge to wisdom? What does it take to make that which I know become that which I feel? What can I do to make the preconscious conscious and create a predisposition to trust rather than a predisposition to withhold trust?

We all must evaluate the honesty, competence, confidence, and authority of those we are engaged with when choosing to offer our trust. Conscious, rational thought remains an essential part of the process. That is not my focus. I am focused on the preconscious. In particular,

I am referring to those elements of the preconscious that shape our attitudes toward risk-taking—the predispositions that craft the questions and establish the hurdle rates that set the table for conscious deliberations. These are the biases, habits, and patterns of thought that influence trust.

Given my observations and experiences among professional investors, it is easy to argue that the intuitive trumps the deliberative the majority of the time. One could spend weeks understanding a stock and months waiting for the right price, but should any series of world events assault our senses on any given day, all that hard work can be sold in the market at a moment's notice. As frustrating as that often feels, the decision to sell may be exactly the right thing to do. Although not intuitively obvious, the spontaneous decision may result from as much preconscious energy and intellect as that which was invested consciously in the stock specific analysis. When I consider all the time I devoted to reading thought pieces, surveying the news, speaking with business leaders and peers, who is to say where the balance of effort and information rests between the conscious and preconscious? I don't know, but I have witnessed countless occasions when the preconscious dictated the decisions made.

When trust, rather than investing, is the subject of discussion, understanding the interplay between preconscious and conscious thought is even more challenging.

Through the course of our lifetime, and the history of lives that preceded ours, we have relentlessly constructed filters and biases within our preconscious that act to censor information received and alter decisions made. Sometimes it feels as if the preconscious is acting as both judge and jury, giving the conscious little room to operate. How free are we to choose? We are only as free as the risks we are willing to take. What risks are we willing to take? We will only take those risks that suit our predispositions for risk. How do we know what risks we are predisposed to take? We know them by dissecting and exposing the hurdle rates we impose. How do we choose the hurdle rates? Hurdle rates are the product of our experiences, memories, and biology. And it is this product that forms the basis of our predispositions to trust and our willingness to trust.

To restore openness, curiosity, balanced risk-taking, and choice, we must examine our memories, be aware of our observations and experiences and understand the clues provided by our subtle biology, in order to expose and challenge our personal biases. We must incorporate projects, strategies and processes into our lives that allow for a culling of these biases and prejudices, restoring the prospect of freedom that is being suffocated by the burdens of our pasts. Charity offers one path to help us unmoor our deeply held biases. But we must take additional steps to permanently dislodge them and free ourselves of these burdens. If we can do this, we will greatly improve our capacity to trust.

Acquiring a more balanced posture toward trust would be a monumental accomplishment. Trust is the social contract we have with ourselves; with our friends, family, and acquaintances; with our institutions; and with our faith. It is the thing that says we have moved from learned knowledge to embraced knowledge. By that, I am referring to that transition when knowledge becomes more than information on a page and transforms into the more deeply held understanding of wisdom. It is the difference between knowing a piece of music versus the ability to improvise.

Knowing is a matter of skill, practice and memory versus improvisation, which is a matter of belief. It's a knowledge that you actually feel rather than know. It comes from a deeper understanding that, for me, can most accurately be described as trust. Those capable in the art of improvisation not only trust themselves and their abilities but they also trust their instincts to follow the music beyond the prescribed notes to places deemed worthy of risk taking. The musician knows that it is there that he or she can find the fertile ground of innovation and greatness. For them, the fear of failing to explore this potential is far more unsettling than the fear of failure itself.

Deeply held trust in oneself and the willingness to trust others is the quality and characteristic that allows a person to be vulnerable, willing to engage without a guarantee of outcome, because a person is not consumed with fear of failure. Rather, he or she is in search of something authentic, durable, and meaningful. This is the great truth to which I aspire and the place where I feel great healing, health, happiness and trust can be found.

IMPECCABLE ACTIONS

B eyond charity, I would like to explore some broad concepts that may help bring you closer to a healthy relationship with trust. The term "impeccable actions" references three skills that can temper bias, elevate experience, and improve the prospect of trust: awareness, acceptance and detachment from outcomes. The common denominator that underscores each of these skills is that they address our ability to fluidly adapt to change.

Change is arguably the only immutable truth that exists in our lives. The friction caused by our failure to recognize, accept, and adapt to change, is an important source of our personal biases. Change presents a fundamental challenge to our increasingly static self-images, leading to feelings of fear and anxiety that lead to the perception of a loss of control. When relentless, disruptive change collides with our self-images, forecasts lose the benefit of dispassionate accuracy, and negative biases become palliative sources of comfort. How we manage change in the context of risk and trust will be the measure of our success. First, we must acquire practices that can selectively help disassemble our webs of personal bias. Then, we must reinforce these practices with strategies that effectively neutralize the impact our biases have on critical, decision-making moments.

AWARENESS

Absolutely nothing can be achieved without awareness. It forms the backbone of our ability to adapt
to change. To develop awareness requires that we navigate a sophisticated armory of our own design, created
to insulate ourselves from awareness because awareness is often uncomfortable. Great awareness asks us to
see both ourselves, and others with nuance and clarity.
Awareness demands that we confront and address the
biases we have created that enable us to manufacture
comfort when comfort is not easily found.

An important tool we call upon to buffer ourselves
from awareness is our habits. We all have built up an
astonishing array of habits to manage our actions, our

emotions, our perceptions, and our responses. At their most harmless, habits allow us to simply disengage from experience. At their most harmful, habits narrow our responses in an effort to avoid risk. The examples are endless. A smoker's habit of lighting a cigarette when faced with an awkward social situation, a frequent drinker's need for alcohol when experiencing stress, the constant checking of phones, Facebook, Twitter, eating sweets, or spending on credit to occupy our quiet moments with distractions. Habits are about drawing straight lines between stimulus and response. They are about making automatic that which should be fluid. They are about making the unpredictable predictable and the stressful without stress.

Habits are windows into the sources of our preconscious bias. They are a strategy useful for regaining a sense of control by engaging in actions and perceptions that are familiar and acceptable. However, when we rely on habits we are actually choosing to withdraw from genuine experience. And by turning away from experience we impair our responses to observed experience and our perceptions of risk lose balance. Soon perceptions of risk become actual risks, we lose our sense of control and our decisions suffer.

When you are anxious about your job performance and you walk outside to smoke, have you come any closer to understanding your anxiety? Have you done anything to improve your performance? Have you done anything to clear your mind and reclaim your energy or enthusiasm? Or have you simply engaged in an unhealthy habit that offers distraction and the false perception of distance from your problems and your feelings?

Control is not gained nor risk reduced by avoiding experience. Risk is intrinsic to all genuine experience. And control is only gained when risk is no longer feared. The more we recoil from risk and the more we detach from genuine experience, the more habits we acquire to accommodate our self-biases and shield our self-images. Gradually, we find ourselves immobilized in a world of constant change, and we acquire postures that withdraw and defend, leading us to become increasingly unaware. However, if we can become increasingly aware of our habits and invest the time required to examine their greater purposes, we have a chance to restore our freedom to choose, awaken our awareness of experience, and ultimately revive our willingness to trust.

In our efforts to pare back habitual behavior, it is not our intention to replace preconscious thought with conscious thought. Rather, the objective is to strip preconscious thought of the burdens of bias. When the preconscious and conscious are free to choose, they conspire in search of best fit. Consider sparring in the martial arts. The gift of the great fighter is not the perfect execution of the punch or the kick. The gift is choice. In every fight, the variables are infinite, and the decision times are short. Strength and skill may be the necessary conditions for being a good fighter, but they are not the sufficient conditions. The great fighter must be versatile and unpredictable. When fighters lead with conscious decision-making, they become wooden, and when fighters lead with preconscious habits, they become predictable. They are in fact hostage to choice, picking and choosing according to prescribed patterns. The great fighters are confident in their skill sets; they see with clarity and respond fluidly. Choice is the authentic product of practice and study. Skills are the necessary condition; choice is the sufficient condition.

Habits are the product of biases, prejudices, and tendencies acquired throughout our lives. We gather them from our families, friends, community, culture, and nationalities. Rules, codes, conventions, and rituals easily morph from guidelines into guide rails that create habits that manage our appearances, our acquaintances, our ideas, and our beliefs. They are the walls that confine our experiences. They are the narrow openings through which we channel our responses. They are powerful because they are about turning off and detaching, when what we must do is turn on and become aware. And they are so dangerous because they live beneath our awareness. They are automatic.

Habits of thought and belief create context and structure through which we process experience. Habits can serve as the voice that rationalizes the thoughts and actions of the racist or function as the advocate inside the head of the politician that makes peace with dishonesty and deception. They are designed to offer us escapes from meaning when meaning proves inconvenient and to release us from the burdens of truth when truth is not easily reconciled.

Consider the religious leader who feels compelled to speak out against science or, in the extreme, deny the existence of dinosaurs. Their entrenched belief in the absolute truth of the biblical story prevents them from accepting any falsity that would shatter the foundations of their commitment. Their habits of belief are so strong that they are incapable of processing any dissonance. This reflexive rigidity of thought stifles curiosity, undermines conversation, and poisons connection. It does not require great imagination to find evidence of such habits in our political beliefs, cultural identities, value systems, or religious dogmas. Habits hijack experience, narrow choice, and distance us from awareness.

Habits place us in conflict with reality by offering us the illusion of freedom from risk. Unfortunately, the risks that are most dangerous are the risks that escape our awareness. Think of simple habits that compromise safety: listening to music when taking a run in the park; holding a phone in one hand and coffee in the other while running across the street to make the light;

standing close to the tracks waiting for the subway to arrive; answering a text while driving. "I like music; it motivates me." "I run here almost every day, it's totally safe." "I hate wasting time." "They can wait." "I want to make sure I get a seat." "The subway is so much safer than it used to be." "I don't want to be left out." "I'll be quick." These are some common habits of behavior that compromise safety by obscuring awareness and creating the illusion of distance from risk when risk is far from distant.

By limiting choice, turning away from risk, and masking awareness, our habits place us in positions of disadvantage when meeting challenges and adapting to change. In business, consider those with whom you exchange ideas, where you source your information, and the methods, skills, and tools you use to solve problems. Over time, practices and people originally considered thoughtful and maybe even innovative become characterized as reliable and reasonable. This is when ideas begin to calcify, information leads to similar conclusions, and methods, tools, and skills atrophy. When habits replace novelty, and challenges are downsized to fit the usual, customary, and reasonable, the light begins to dim.

We have habits that narrow our social experiences by limiting the groups we form, the places we frequent, and the sites we visit. We even create habits that serve to limit our potential. Rather than expose ourselves to the uncertainty of real experience, we choose to identify and attach ourselves to the pleasing stability of images, symbols, and ideas. Are we great athletes because we cheer for a team that wins the title? Are we sexy because we drive a high-performance sports car? Are we powerful because we live in a nation with a strong military? Are we number one because we shout along with the crowd? By engaging in this form of deception, we distance ourselves from awareness, lose the courage to question and compromise our ability to skillfully adapt. We effectively exchange the potential of imagination, curiosity, and discovery for the false sense of stability offered by the symbol or the image. Ideas seem to be easier to digest than reality and symbols are so much more stable than facts. We run from risk in exchange for habits that guard and inflate our carefully curated self-images. We prefer the impression of the sure thing versus the expression of the thing not yet known.

We try to know ourselves by cataloging our titles earned, credits accumulated, and objects acquired. We try and make fixed that which should be fluid. As a result, we make it increasingly difficult to adapt to change. The habits of identification and attachment are designed to help us hold on when life demands that we let go and evolve. Does business ask us to solve problems already solved? Or must we evolve to meet the next set of challenges and conditions? Do relationships become richer by reliving the past? Or must we find new sources of richness to feed our changing interests, desires, and abilities? Does an aging athlete remain vital by trying to reacquire the physical skills of prior years? Or perhaps is it best that he or she learn to exploit intellect and experience in search of new sources of advantage? Life is in front of us. Habits urge us to look back.

Habits direct our actions, change how we think, and even co-opt how we feel. They have the power to regulate our emotions, scripting responses to moments that should ordinarily be beyond our capacity to control: "I need to be strong. I can't show weakness. I can't let them know how I really feel."

Habits are at war with shame, vulnerability, and weakness, and by being so, they place us at war with empathy, crippling genuine connection and marginalizing our humanity. Many think of habits as small and innocuous. But, when habits are inspected under the bright lights, you begin to understand the degree to which they shape and define our lives. Plotting a life with fewer habits is no small achievement.

Meditation is the training platform that teaches us how to become increasingly aware of our selves, our habits, and the world around us. Meditation teaches the practitioner to dispassionately observe thoughts as they enter consciousness and then let them pass gently out of consciousness without judgment. The idea is to become aware of our thoughts and then detach from these thoughts. When the fundamental identity of the meditator is no longer attached to the thought, the thought loses its emotional charge. As this separation becomes more practiced, the attachment to thoughts becomes more distant, and the accompanying emotional context of thoughts begins to fade. Because negative thoughts are the most emotionally complex thoughts held in memory, they are the memories most likely to lose valence. And because negative memories are more closely aligned with risk aversion, they are more likely to be sources of bias. As these memories lose priority, so do the accompanying biases, requiring fewer habits to express and act on these same biases.

I have read that mindfulness—the awareness that comes from the practice of meditation—is a rebellion against the agenda of natural selection because natural selection is all about advancing the self. What I would argue is that our predisposition for self-bias is powerful, and mindfulness offers the prospect of détente with the self, rather than some form of rebellion. With less focus on the self come less biases, implying fewer habits and offering more space to connect.

As we train and practice meditation, we become increasingly aware. And as we take those awareness skills beyond our scripted, quiet places, we begin to expose the habits that consume our lives. Once you identify them, try to disrupt the simplest habits. Brush your teeth or comb your hair with the other hand. Feel the amount of thought and energy invested in these small habits. Then consider the energy invested in the larger habits of perception, emotion, and belief.

Bring a magnifying glass to your life. Ask questions of thoughts and statements that formerly were not exposed to scrutiny. Search for the origin of your habits. Dissect their applications and purposes. Begin to intentionally break a few habits for short periods of time. Imagine what might be possible if all the energy invested in habits were released. Why are they important? What would you do in their absence? How do they shape your life? Begin to observe the habits of others to help gain insight into your own process of discovery.

I will admit that, amid the clutter and clamor of our daily grinds, staying truly aware is no small challenge. But I would like to alert you to an experience that we all visit with surprising regularity that offers a unique opportunity to explore habits and biases.

There is a newly identified area of neurological function referred to as "mind wandering." Apparently, mind wandering uses a unique pathway in the brain called the default mode network and this network can be active for almost 50 percent of our waking moments. The research is still in early days, but some of the first findings associate the network with the acts of reflection (looking back) and planning (looking forward). In other words, we may actually spend half our waking moments ruminating over the past to organize our lives going forward.

So my logic is as follows: if negatively biased experience dominates memory, then it should also dominate our thoughts when reviewing the past and planning for the future. If this is so, then when our default mode networks are active, so will be the biases that emerge from negative memories, as well as the habits constructed in support of our biases. If we are aware during periods of mind wandering, our habits will be on display for examination and challenge.

Clearly, few of us are aware of how much we daydream and how active our minds are during this process. If we remain unaware, we become victims of a reinforcing cycle of negative bias, habit formation, and habit reinforcement. But if we can train ourselves to become more aware of the times, places, and circumstances when our minds tend to wander, we place ourselves in position to reframe the power invested in the exact negative thoughts and patterns that occupy positions of priority in our memories. And if that is possible, we put ourselves in position to deconstruct the habits that shape our lives.

I tend to characterize moments of mind wandering as the times when I hear that voice in my head and when I sometimes talk things out with myself. I have noticed that this happens with great frequency when I am walking my dog or taking a shower. As I have become more practiced at identifying these moments, I use this time to quiet my mind, become very aware of the present recollections, and take account of any habits and biases I can identify. Once aware, I pause to examine their underlying intentions and meanings, after which I let the thoughts pass without judgment or attachment. Effectively, I try to convert moments of mind wandering into moments of meditation and awareness. It may not be the romanticized version of meditation, but it certainly moves you in the right direction.

When a compelling thought arises during mind wandering, and you have reached a place that allows you to recognize and step away from the thought, pause and begin to ask questions. Why did this thought resurface? Why is it important? What actions were taken? What judgments and decisions were made? Why was this experience classified as negative? What were the consequences? What were the unintended consequences? What needs to be learned? What needs to be changed? Why is this experience still compelling?

For example, if a thought arises concerning a failed investment in the stock market, I might ask myself, "Why did this thought arise? What cues or triggers are in my immediate environment that may have caused me revisit this thought? What emotions are attached to this thought; anger, sadness, or possibly fear?" While I ask myself these questions I stay very aware of my body to feel for clues or reactions that may indicate that I am moving closer to the truth.

If I were to determine that I was angry, I may ask; "Was I angry with myself or was I angry with another? Or was I angry with myself because I was angry with someone else and I failed to take responsibility for my choices? Was I angry about the quality of my work or the effort invested? Was I upset about the financial loses or were these loses a convenient cover for other more fundamental concerns or issues? And if that was the case, what might these issues really be?"

This is a sample dialogue to help you start the process. It is not a script. You will need to experiment to develop the line of questioning that leads you closer to something that may resemble the truth. But I challenge you to try and stay in touch with your body to help gain direction. As we previously discussed, risk is visceral. And this process is all about taking risk. So if you are really challenging yourself, going to places that make you truly uncomfortable, you will feel it. Just as you will feel the incredible sensations of calmness and contentment when you confront and address issues of great personal meaning and consequences.

You know you are getting somewhere when you allow yourself to be painfully vulnerable. I call it "splitting the atom." It is that feeling that you have pressed this thing as far as you can take it. Remember those moments when a curious young child ceaselessly asked "Why?" Consider the cleverness behind this line of inquiry. The child only understands things at the most elemental level. Self-image and bias have yet to cloud their picture. To quote Albert Einstein, "If you can't explain it to a six-year-old, you don't understand it yourself." Think of yourself as the six-year-old child in search of answers you can understand. When he or she may understand, then so might you. And when you reach this place, take a moment to expose the biases, habits, and intentions that caused this thought to impose itself on your quiet mind. And then let the thought go without judgment or attachment.

It took a while to improve my awareness. It took far longer to willingly be sufficiently vulnerable to reveal meaning. Having finally arrived at a better place, I move thoughts from awareness to meaning fairly quickly. And when thoughts repeat, I begin from a far more fundamental place and conclude with far greater insight. In time, many habits and biases have lost their teeth. But most importantly, my perspective of that which would normally be considered negative has changed radically.

Before an event or piece of information can be negatively biased, it must be characterized as negative. In time, what I have observed through this process is that very little is either purely negative or positive. Most often the thoughts seem closer to shades of gray. For example, I originally characterized my A-Fib as an extremely negative change of circumstances. Now I am not so sure. If you recall, I was training like a twenty year old when I was over fifty. On the surface it was pretty easy to argue that I was simply unwilling to gracefully accept my age. But there were deeper issues that required my attention. And after years of awareness training, thoughtful examination and relentless challenges to my carefully crafted brand of convention, I have found a place of far greater ease and happiness. I can't say I am glad I have A-Fib. But I can say with absolute certainty that I am glad that I have changed. And without the burdens and demands attached to this condition, I am certain that I would not have been able to summon the resolve and commitment necessary to make these changes lasting.

My changed perspective has changed the way I respond to experience, and fewer experiences seem to warrant the bias and priority they were once given. As a consequence, my relationship with risk has changed. I am less quick to categorize and more willing to explore. Less judgment has led to more genuine experience, more genuine experience has been a source of greater awareness, and greater awareness has resulted in fewer habits.

There is an old Chinese story that is designed to teach this evolution of perspective. A little boy on his sixteenth birthday was given a horse. Everybody in the village spoke of the boy's good fortune except the Zen master who, when asked, replied, "We will see." Later, the boy fell from the horse and broke his leg. All bemoaned the boy's bad luck except the Zen master who said, "We will see." Later, war broke out, and all the young men in the village were forced to enlist except the boy with the broken leg. People said, "Oh, what good fortune the boy has," only to hear the Zen master say, "We will see." Nothing is clearly good, and nothing is clearly bad. In time, we will see. And this is how it evolved for me with my health challenges. And with this new perspective, I believe bias will play a smaller role in my life going forward.

Challenging biases and habits is incredibly difficult. The process asks you to question the most important assumptions used in the construction of your life. But if you meet with any degree of success, the rewards are more than worthy compensation for all your efforts. Developing the willingness to be truly vulnerable and highly aware will change the content and character of your experiences and thus will change your basic relationship with risk. And when your attitudes and disposition toward risks change, so will change the choices you make as well as the direction of your life. Habits and biases are about dictating the questions we are forced to ask. Developing the skills of awareness and inquiry are about reacquiring the power to ask the questions of our choosing.

If our default mode networks are active as frequently as some scientists have suggested, then, when failing to act, we become victims of a self-reinforcing cycle that will likely lead to greater bias and more habits of thought and action. With awareness, we give ourselves the opportunity to change the inevitable and restore a balanced posture toward trust.

Our human design is infinitely sophisticated and the rationale supportive of the vast majority of the friction between preconscious thought and conscious thought is far beyond question. Really, how much debate should be permitted when a bear attacks, when a mugger wants your wallet, or maybe even when your girlfriend says, "I love you"? What I wish to draw attention to are the moments when self-bias ends and self-image begins; when forecasts are replaced by expectations; when pessimism or optimism dictates choice; when prejudice, judgment, or habit is convenient; or when opinion rises above observation and fact. Maybe the key is not what or how much you accomplish. Maybe the more important achievement is that you become aware, actively engaging in a process that can reduce bias and restore real choice.

With greater awareness, you gain knowledge of the filters and biases that influence decisions, and you acquire the power to choose a different path. You can become the traffic cop at this critical intersection between the conscious and the preconscious. And you are given the chance to add your voice to the information that moves forward and that which should slow down.

There is a story told about when wise men approached the Buddha and asked, "Sir, are you a god?" Buddha replied, "No, I am not a god." Then, they asked, "Are you a man?" Buddha replied, "No, I am not a man." So the wise men asked, "Then what are you?" The Buddha said, "I am awake!"

Awakening involves making one's actions conscious and intentional as opposed to automatic and habitual. Fundamentally creating a life with fewer habits and without the accompanying illusion of control is a far more sustaining way to live.

ACCEPTANCE

Learning to accept change is an enormous struggle because change is oftentimes unpredictable, and unpredictability is emotionally untenable. Our survival is dependent on our capacity to make accurate predictions. It is this unique ability that enabled us to be such efficient hunters when our prey was often more physically gifted than ourselves. However, when the accuracy of our forecasts suffers, when that which we understand about ourselves and the changing environment ceases to be in harmony, we become anxious and confused, and we simply fail to function. In the extreme, we have all witnessed examples when animals or people find themselves so overwhelmed with circumstances that they become immobilized and shut down.

To address this problem, we have two choices: either improve our predictions or improve our responses to predictions. Improving predictions is a highly complex matter of awareness, maturity, instinct, intellect, and physicality. It is an integral part of our personal growth, and improving this ability is a matter of comprehensive individual development. General remedies would likely be of little value. However, changing a person's response to predictions is a matter of perception and emotion. Fortunately, in this case, general remedies can have tremendous value.

It might be reasonable to question the value of picking up the pieces after the fact. What good is remedy when one's prediction has already failed? Nothing can be further from the truth. We are all visited by cycles of success and failure. When one's business is thriving, poor health visits. When one is at the top of one's game, injury visits. When one feels most secure, tragedy visits. When one feels most fortunate, one is visited by the greater fortune of others. Life offers ceaseless challenges. We are challenged from within and challenged from without. And the measure of greatest success and happiness may be much more closely aligned with how we deal with failure rather than how often we are fortunate enough to count our successes. How we respond to failure is the measure of one's resilience, and resilience may be our most valuable ally in life. Any steps we can take toward greater resilience will pay significant dividends toward improving our ability to learn, grow, predict, and decide, all of which will create a healthy framework for improving our ability to trust.

To improve our responses to predictions, we must turn our attention to the close cousin of predictions: expectations. A prediction is more closely aligned with the less emotionally involved act of anticipation versus an expectation, which is a prediction invested with emotion. When a prediction loses dispassion, the prediction morphs into an expectation. And it is expectations, not predictions that comprise the fertile ground from which stress, anxiety, and fear gain strength, undermining our resilience and impairing our ability to respond.

Prediction is grounded in observation and response. Think of the moment when the driver of an oncoming vehicle suddenly swerved into your lane. Your prediction of the person's behavior was incorrect, and your response was immediate. There was no review or disappointment. You simply reacted. Expectations, however, are far less surgical executions of peering forward. Expectations account for observations and patterns but also take into consideration the demands of self-image. As such, expectations incorporate the hopes and dreams of their manufacturers, opening the door for bias, inaccuracy, and misplaced motivation. Think about it. If a prediction proves inaccurate, it is a failed prediction.

When an expectation proves inaccurate, the failure is assigned to you. And with that distinction comes all the baggage and burdens that consume our attention and distract us from the tasks ahead.

Now, consider what happens when an expectation proves wrong. When constructing an earnings outlook for a stock I own, I often find it very difficult to detach the estimates from my hopes and desires for profit. Accordingly, estimates are often tainted with biases that would be supportive of higher stock prices, obscuring my clear vision of reality. If my estimates prove overly optimistic and the stock performance does not respond as expected, I am likely to become frustrated, disappointed, and defensive. Further action is now hostage to my need to review rather than my need to react to the present. Unfortunately, as you are likely aware, hesitation and doubt, are typically accompanied by loss in the stock market.

It's odd. The notion of a hope, dream, or expectation is somewhat expansive as you consider what might be. But, in effect, they tend to make your view smaller. They actually serve to shrink the range of acceptable outcomes to suit the outcome imagined.

Expectations present additional, complicating features. The design of an expectation often takes into consideration the perceptions and judgments of others because expectations are also invested in the way we wish others to see ourselves. Effectively, expectations function as our own personal advertising or public relations agencies: "If this stock earns what I expect, I will be rich." "If I give a lot of money to charity, I hope to earn the respect of my peers." "If I get this deal done, I believe they will consider me for that big promotion." Expectations are far more psychologically complex than predictions, and they divert attention from a clear understanding of the present moment.

When expectations are at odds with reality, attention shifts to managing the past rather than acting in the present. Any effort expended to align past experience with self-image is a waste of precious personal resources. With our personal compasses fixed on resolving any challenge to our self-esteem, we are no longer in position to skillfully adapt. What was once a failed prediction—providing facts and information to plot the next course of action—becomes a matter of personal loss, creating feelings of insecurity, sadness, and disappointment. Facts and information are obscured, and the act of anticipating the next move devolves into an emotional exercise in search of validation. Inevitably, the predictions that follow are compromised as we turn our gaze backward in the hope of reconciling the past, while reality ceaselessly marches forward. The results are obvious: we lag hopelessly behind the curve, compounding our errors.

I can't possibly count the number of times I have watched seasoned investment professionals absolutely freeze in the face of falling markets and mounting client losses. What will their clients think? What will their peers think? What will their bosses think? How will they rebound from these disasters? If they were capable of detaching themselves from their expectations, their attention would turn from reconciling the past to profiting from the present. Once a financial advisor is consumed by his or her sense of failure, he or she is no longer capable of processing new opportunities and, more importantly, evaluating upcoming risks. The number one job of all financial advisors is to help his or her clients manage risks. But the funny thing about risk is that it doesn't exist in the past. Risk only exists in the future. And when an advisor is trapped in the past, he or she is no longer capable of fulfilling their principle responsibility to clients, helping them navigate financial risk.

The damage described by this pattern of expectation-driven behavior is not isolated to the single failed expectation. The perception of personal failure that accompanies unrealized expectations is invested with considerable emotional charge, creating more negative memories, stored with great priority. These then become the memories that form the basis of an increased number of biases and habits. With more habits comes a narrower view of the present, limiting options and impairing decisions.

Expectations are our vehicle for controlling experience rather than observing and participating in experience. It is our way of sanitizing experience to create the illusion of security. Oddly, it accomplishes the very opposite. Expectations force observation through the filter of personal perspective. They alter decisions to fit within the confines of a construction that may have little to do with observed experience. Expectations are the tools with which we try to manufacture experience or try to manufacture our perceptions of experience, rather than simply participating in experience.

In the movie *A Time to Kill*, a white lawyer is charged with defending a heartbroken black father who avenged the brutal rape of his ten year old daughter by shooting the two white men who have openly admitted to having committed the crime. The story takes place in a small segregated southern town with a history of racially biased justice. At the conclusion of his closing argument, the defense lawyer asks the white jury to close their eyes as he takes them through the details of the horrible crime. When his story reaches its climax, he pauses dramatically, then asks the white jury to imagine the crime as if the little girl was instead white. The courtroom takes a moment to catch its collective breath.

You can't change a deeply held bias or prejudice with a single remark. But you can change an expectation rooted in bias or prejudice. By shattering expectations and exposing the jurors to a reality separate from their personal perspective, the lawyer was able reframe how the jury processed the facts of the case. Temporarily, the filters were removed and the facts and circumstances of the case were newly processed. By simply removing the jurors' personal expectations, observations were processed with new perspectives, decisions changed, and one man who committed an act of violence was set free while two others were convicted.

From the broadest point of perspective, predictions are tools that can be used to exact future gains through the examination of the ever-changing present. This is radically different from expectations, which are tools that can be used to create the impression of present gains before we experience the ever-changing future. Expectations are the equivalent of cashing and spending a check before it has been issued. If, for some reason, the check fails to arrive, there are debts to pay above and beyond the loss of the check. By psychologically counting gains before they have been realized, we put ourselves at remarkable disadvantage. By expecting gains, we have effectively tried to turn away from risk, and by doing so have left ourselves more exposed. When circumstances vary from plan, risk compounds, and we feel trapped. We become prisoners of the past, handcuffed by our needs to expect.

If one were able to sever his or her need to convert predictions into expectations, one's relationship with change would permanently be altered because change would, by definition, no longer be unexpected. As stated by a great aikido master, the idea is to become skilled at coming back, not holding on. The more we practice returning to center, the more we achieve balance in everyday life. Thus, the goal is to become fluid in your attitudes and responses in a world in which the fundamental is constant change.

In order to part ways with our need to create expectations, we must again call upon our awareness skills. In my experience, I have found this exercise accessible because the habit of investing predictions with the emotions necessary to create expectations comes with very specific language. *I expect, I hope, I dream, I believe, I suppose, I think, I assume,* and *I imagine* are some of the more common phrases used to signal this habit. And fortunately, when we are engaged in these acts of personal advertisement and assurance, we are often accompanied by the voices in our head that are energized and engaged, actively massaging the difference between observed reality and our personal needs. With both specific language and self-talk, there are many cues to alert the aware observer.

If you can deliberately disrupt the habit of expectation building, you can begin to appreciate the important role that expectations play in your planning processes. When I first began this exercise, I tried to identify the subject matter in which expectations were most frequently used. Then, I thought about the frequently used trigger language I relied upon. In my case, the most frequently visited topic was stock performance, and the most frequently used phrases were "I expect" and "I bet." Identifying the moments when you create expectations is not as complicated as you might imagine. For instance, I can never recall going to the grocery store thinking "I bet the fruit will be fresh today," because the condition of the fruit is simply not that important to me. However, when a matter is worthy of expectation, I am deeply engaged. There is a lot of personal capital on the line when I choose to create an expectation. Never fail to underestimate the importance of a forecast that involves self-image.

With characteristics such as emotional intensity, risk, and planning, it should not be surprising to associate the formation of expectations with moments of mind wandering. Attention to those moments when mind wandering is most common can also serve an important purpose in helping with the task of identifying, disrupting, and dissecting the habitual use of expectations. Thus, before walking the dog, I take a moment to alert myself to be self-observant. It's fascinating how easy it is to lose track of self-observation. And on such occasions, when self-observation stifles mind wandering, I find that I tend to be somewhat more vigilant through the course of the day. When I finally recognize the use of the trigger language, I take a moment to deconstruct the attached thought. I remove the language from the thought and explore how the language changed my intention. What I typically find is that the language re-directs the intention away from the original subject of the thought.

Let's explore using one of my stock market examples. I'm walking the dog and I catch myself rehearsing the following thought: "After all my research I expect that this stock will go up at least 20 percent on Tuesday, when they announce earnings of one dollar." When I attach the phrase "I expect" to this thought, I have attached my ego to the prediction. Now all of my efforts, all of my thought processes and all that I think of myself will be on the line. And should the stock decline next Tuesday when they report earnings of one dollar, my first reaction would be to think about *my* disappointment and *my* poor decision, rather than focus on the changed circumstances of the company and stock price.

Alternatively, if the phrase had been constructed as "This stock will go up at least 20 percent next Tuesday when they report one dollar," the statement is objectively constructed, and the focus stays with the earnings and the stock price movement. I am no longer the subject of the thought. My personal investment of time, effort and money is now separated from my observations and analyses of the reported earnings and stock price movement, allowing me the room needed to capitalize on success or mitigate losses. It is a subtle change, but it is by no means minor. If the company does not report one dollar or the stock fails to rise at least 20 percent, I am now free to react to the change rather than to reframe the change in the context of my personal needs and desires.

In my experience, when someone is preoccupied with self-examination and rationalization, that is the moment when an analytical exercise changes into a speculative exercise. In truth, if my prediction proves wrong, I should accept that the investment was beyond my complete understanding. If that is the case, I should quickly come to terms with the fact that I am operating somewhat in the dark and should exit the investment. If I am not willing to accept this reality and choose to hold the stock, I am accepting levels of risk beyond my understanding, and that is never wise.

The decision to buy, sell, or hold a particular stock may actually include many more considerations. But regardless of the complexity, the central truth remains the same. When I enter into an expectation, the decision process loses important objectivity. Maybe I was having a tough year in the stock market and I needed this stock to rise? Maybe I had gotten other investors into this investment and could not face their disappointment? The larger point worth noting is that when the self is removed, bias is greatly diminished. With less bias we gain greater clarity and are required to negotiate fewer impediments to pure response. When the Mercedes veers toward your car, you never stop and think, "I can't imagine that a person in such a nice car would do such a thing." You just respond.

Once you adjust the language of the forecast, you are better positioned to examine the subject with greater clarity and act with authority. Additionally, this exercise offers you the distance needed to understand motivation and expose important psychological needs that require your further attention. You begin to appreciate how importantly emotions can alter the dynamics of a question requiring a judgment of risk.

To ignore this is both naive and perilous. I am not trying to advocate a lack of connection with emotions. At its core, this book is actually advocating for more emotional availability and connection. But I am arguing that emotions can also be voices through which bias can be expressed, and bias can be corrosive to risk appraisal, decision-making, and trust. Locating the borders of these subtle differences is the art that will come with practice and increased awareness.

With consistent effort, identifying the habitual use of expectations becomes easier, deconstructing the language becomes simpler, and reconstructing the intention becomes clearer. Mind wandering is simply one example. With practice, your personal antennae will get more and more sensitive. And as you increasingly become aware of your habit of using the language of expectations, you can begin to slowly unwind the patterns. The remedy is simply a matter of practice. For me, it's no different than exercising. I never liked doing it, but I always viewed the psychic and physical rewards to be of such great value that it was relatively easy to make a consistent commitment. If you can visualize the rewards of a life with fewer expectations allowing for less stress, less anxiety, less fear, more options, and better decision-making, then commitment may not be so difficult.

DETACHMENT FROM OUTCOMES

S imply stated, these are actions done without regard to outcome. By detaching from outcomes, you position yourself to commit your full force and energy to that which you think is right. As a result, two important qualities emerge. First, you become consumed with the task rather than the expectations of results. If you have ever played golf, just try and guide the ball onto the fairway. Your swing is quickly compromised, and the ball is nowhere to be found. However, if you take aim for the fairway and then lose track of the outcome, focusing on creating a complete swing with your full force and energy, the outcome is far more pleasing. You must create a disposition that the outcome is nothing more than a byproduct of an action done well.

Secondly, by diminishing the importance of outcomes, you diminish the importance attached to your actions. As a result, should the action or outcome be less than ideal, you are well adjusted and prepared to plot your next best course of action, raising the probability of future success. A person consumed with the expectations of results must first address the failure before he or she can move on. Additionally, their actions become tainted with the emotion of failure. Doubt and lack of confidence unnecessarily compromise future results. The person of impeccable action does not suffer this burden and is quicker, clearer, and more confident in his or her response. Impeccable actions are actions wrapped up in the constantly evolving present. This posture frees you of the attachments and expectations that serve little purpose beyond fostering disappointment and confusion.

Imagine someone who is highly sensitive to even the smallest changes. Then, imagine that same person who readily accepts change and is quick to address it. Lastly, consider the person who is willing to commit to thought and action without fear and compromise. It is now easy to imagine a person of great resilience. If you are capable of seeing yourself as resilient, I believe that you can completely change your relationship with yourself.

Fear and anxiety lose much of their power, and for the first time, you can truly learn to trust yourself. And the very act of trusting yourself further reinforces your resilience. This puts you in a far better position to gain the trust of others as well as to share your trust with them. Importantly, if you can do this, you will have fundamentally reshaped your relationship with the world, freeing yourself of the false burdens of managing and protecting, and offering yourself the possibility of engaging the future with curiosity, courage, and competence.

CLOSING THOUGHTS

I n my experience, reading and writing about this process was far different from the actual experience.
Elegant phrases and logical designs were often replaced
by grueling lessons learned at considerable personal
cost. Without tenacity, vulnerability, and adaptability,
none of this would have been possible.

After working with my new naturopath for about two
years, my response to her course of therapy was amazing. Evidence of irregular heartbeats was largely gone.
As my diagnosis improved, I steadily increased my levels
of physical fitness training. Visions of reclaiming my old
self were finally imaginable, and I was anxious to move
the process forward. Then, one evening, I was awakened

in the middle of the night by excruciating pain in my chest, shoulder, and rib cage. Fortunately, I had an appointment with my naturopath the next morning. When I arrived, many of the symptoms were still present, and after taking my readings, she was clearly alarmed. She had not seen this level of distress since our early days. This was very tough to swallow. After a short exam, she strongly urged me to immediately go to the hospital for blood work, where they could provide us with results quickly.

This turn of events was completely surprising. I went to the hospital, but I refused to accept her concern of a pending heart attack. After the blood draw was finished, I decided to visit my craniosacral therapist, Dr. T., whose office was nearby. I explained the situation and argued my case for muscle pain that was attributable to a series of new, strenuous exercises. In response to my direction, he began massaging and manipulating the areas of concern. In the past, such therapy usually resulted in fairly immediate relief, but this time, the result was the most debilitating pain I had ever experienced. Breathing became tremendously painful. I had to end the session shortly thereafter and unwisely drove myself home.

I remember calling my wife to the garage to help me into the house, and once in bed, I realized that something was desperately wrong. A couple of hours later, Dr. T. came by the house to administer additional therapy, but there was little he could do to alleviate the pain. The blood tests were not due until the next day, so I decided to hunker down for the night and try to rest. My pain threshold had always been high, but as I lay in bed, breathing was testing my limits. As the evening wore on, the pain continued to escalate, and Lisa decided it was time to go to the emergency room. The threat of a heart attack received priority when we arrived, and I was immediately moved into the main hospital for further examination. After the battery of tests were completed, the doctors cleared me of a heart attack and instead told me that I had a pleural effusion, which is a buildup of excess fluid in the area between the chest and lung cavities. They didn't think it was serious and thought it would clear up gradually on its own. They sent me home with some painkillers, and after a few days of rest, I was okay.

As I reflected on the situation, it was obvious that I was the catalyst for this whole cascade of events. I was more anxious to reclaim the past than I was appreciative of my present circumstances. Rather than accept my improving health as a new beginning, I tried to capitalize on it to relive the familiar. The new exercises I had incorporated into my routine were designed to build punching power that would be useful in my karate classes. When the pain surfaced in these same areas, I presumed that massage therapy would provide the relief

I required. Unfortunately, this was exactly the wrong remedy and as a result, the pain escalated rapidly. As a consequence of my actions and my direction of therapy, what may have been a temporary problem mushroomed into something larger. And now, I found myself back in the condition I had struggled with two years earlier. To make matters worse, my naturopath later informed me that she was leaving private practice. My safety net was once again severed.

In the past, my reaction to such a turn of events would have been very predictable. Blame and self-judgment were sure to follow feelings of anger at having thrown away two years of hard work to appease my vain wishes. Accusation, isolation, and doubt would precede a sense of depression and failure that would end with a decision to simply give up. But this time, that didn't happen. I was mad, but the scale of emotion was very different from prior responses. I immediately got the name of a new naturopath; I continued to read with purpose and genuinely made an effort to learn from my mistakes rather than use them as a rationale for declaring defeat.

I had learned something of extraordinary value. Although some of the measurable signs I monitored had regressed meaningfully, I was resolute in my determination to go forward. Several years later, I have improved but have yet to reach the statistical heights I had previously achieved. But when viewed from a different angle,

I have surpassed previous highs because I have proven to be more resilient. For the first time, I trust that things will be okay, and that speaks to the possibility of durable change.

This book was a byproduct of my search for remedy from my serious health problem and the overpowering sense of loss that preoccupied my thoughts and disposition. As I climbed out from my bunker, I began to understand the extraordinary complexity and raw pain required to see oneself with some degree of clarity. I began to come to terms with the many obstacles one must navigate to arrive at a place where lessons learned can comfortably merge with a readiness to receive those lessons.

Ironically, many years ago, I faced some of the very same questions that are the subject of this book. After two years of dating, I had taken my girlfriend to the Hamptons for a romantic spring getaway. As we were enjoying our last dinner before returning to New York City, she delivered the dagger: "Where is this relationship going?" After doing my best Muhammad Ali bob-and-weave imitation, I found myself no closer to escaping this dreaded question. Finally, I relented. I asked how long I had, and was told six months. It was go time.

I spent every bit of the next six months grinding on this question. I consulted with everyone. I processed every variable, tested every counterargument and certainly explored alternatives. As time was running short and no change in timeline could be negotiated, I happened upon an observation that made all the difference in the world. I realized that Lisa was the only girl I had ever dated whose opinion I actively solicited concerning matters of great personal importance. I wanted her advice. In fact, I *needed* her advice. I trusted her. And that was far too valuable to lose. I got the ring, we went to Bermuda, and I proposed on the last day of my six-month trial period. It was the best decision I ever made. She is the unsung heroine of this story. And it is a tribute that her contributions to my health and happiness were so consistently present, powerful and subtle that they may not have made for interesting reading. But without them I would be forever lost.

I had really figured it out. Trust was the centerpiece of a good marriage. It was also the centerpiece of a relationship that has provided comfort, security, and joy. Unfortunately, the insight stopped there. I had made one of the great discoveries of my life. I had unlocked one of life's great mysteries, but I was unaware of what I had learned. At the time, "trust" was the answer to a single question, not the answer to a lifetime of questions yet to be asked. It was disposable. I did not see its broader, transformative value. I was not yet at a place where lessons learned could merge with my readiness to learn lessons.

Many years later, things seem to have changed. Finally, the tidal wave of expectations and judgments that was built up through the course of a lifetime has begun to recede. And for the first time, I was ready to see the bigger picture. And maybe more importantly, I was ready to learn.

At the center of this place of discovery, I began to understand the seismic impact that trust has had on my life. I began to appreciate the pivotal role it would occupy as I began to challenge and change my prospects for living a happier and healthier life. And I came to realize how few people recognized this central truth. This is a subject of paramount importance. This is a subject that should command the highest levels of priority in our family conversations, in our schools, in our businesses, and in the institutions that impact our lives.

The desire to connect has now transformed into the requirement to connect, as we navigate a world of increasing pace and complexity. And the glue that securely binds connection is trust. We must all navigate the burdens of change by ourselves, but if we don't join in secure alliances with others in all matters of life, from personal to professional, we are unlikely to navigate change in a deeply meaningful and truly successful way. Our ability to trust faces unprecedented challenge in our modern, technological world. Unless we truly understand the complex nature of the competing forces that impact trust, we have little chance to stem the steady decline we all so deeply feel.

We are a winning-obsessed culture. We wildly over-rate success and overly punish failure. Rather than admit defeat, we reframe endlessly in an effort to protect our selves and those we love from failure. We do it in the media, we do it in politics, we do it with our laws, we do it with our social policy, we do it with our military policy, we do it in our places of work, we do it in sports, we do it with our celebrities, we do it with our kids, and we sure do it with ourselves. As a result of our fear of failure, we have become institutionally and socially engineered to be risk-averse. With a lower tolerance for risk comes a more cautious attitude toward sharing our trust. With less trust comes less freedom of choice, making change more difficult to negotiate.

As plans stray from script, we increasingly turn inward and rely on the comfort of convention. As the great economist John Maynard Keynes once said, "Worldly wisdom teaches that it is better for reputation to fail conventionally than to succeed unconventionally." As our choices narrow, and our reliance on habitual response grows, the quality of outcomes suffers. Fear begets fear, and our instincts call us to double down on our efforts to inoculate ourselves from failure. In response, we erect walls and create boundaries, fostering bias, dishonesty, and a collapse of trust.

Greg Lewin

Ultimately, every transaction we engage in, every relationship and emotion we share, and every belief we hold dear, is predicated on trust—the trust of authenticity, the trust of reciprocity, and the trust of fairness. Without trust, we are forced back to a solitary, fear-based existence. I have heard people argue that trust is not the question. They argue that trustworthiness is all that matters. Offering trust to those deemed trustworthy is always appropriate, and withholding trust from those not worthy is equally important. This may be obvious, but there exists a question of greater fundamental importance. Are we in position to properly and fairly judge trustworthiness when our minds are operating in highly self-biased and negatively biased modes? Are we adequately aware of the storm of preconscious bias that greatly influences conscious choice? Have the cues, interactions, and patterns we were designed to interpret become so incomprehensible in our modern existence that we have compromised our capacities to properly evaluate trustworthiness and then offer our trust?

My intention in writing this book was to be aware of science but not hostage to science. I know that I took many liberties and made many leaps of faith. But within the context of my resources, I wanted to provide sufficient guidance and evidence worthy of starting a far broader conversation. I believe that this should be the next big topic of focus. There is not a single person or facet of life that does not require a greater appreciation of this prime, moving force. This is a matter central to our progress. This is a matter central to our happiness. This is a matter central to our survival. This is a matter of trust.

ABOUT THE AUTHOR

Greg Lewin has spent thirty years on Wall Street as a technology analyst, institutional salesman, and fund manager. He is also the founder of the American Dream Project, an organization that united hundreds of New York City's most challenged students with some of the city's most powerful businesses and their dedicated employees. The project gained national recognition and was honored by President George H.W. Bush.

Lewin received a bachelor's degree in engineering from Northwestern University and an MBA from New York University. He is a third-degree black belt and enjoys spending time with his two children and his wife of twenty-five years.

Greglewin1957@gmail.com
www.facebook.com/officialgreglewin
www.linkedin.com/in/g1lewin